New Directions for
Institutional Research

Gloria Crisp

EDITOR

Using Qualitative
Research to Promote
Organizational
Intelligence

Ezekiel Kimball

Karla I. Loya

EDITORS

Number 174
Jossey-Bass
San Francisco

Using Qualitative Research to Promote Organizational Intelligence
Ezekiel Kimball and Karla I. Loya (eds.)
New Directions for Institutional Research, no. 174
Editor: Gloria Crisp

NEW DIRECTIONS FOR INSTITUTIONAL RESEARCH, (Print ISSN: 0271-0579; Online ISSN: 1536-075X), is published quarterly by W
Subscription Services, Inc., a Wiley Company, 111 River St., Hoboken, NJ 07030-5774 USA.

Postmaster: Send all address changes to *NEW DIRECTIONS FOR INSTITUTIONAL RESEARCH*, John Wiley & Sons Inc., C/O The Sherid
Press, PO Box 465, Hanover, PA 17331 USA.

Information for subscribers

NEW DIRECTIONS FOR INSTITUTIONAL RESEARCH is published in 4 issues per year. Institutional subscription prices for 2017 are:
Print & Online: US$461 (US), US$515 (Canada & Mexico), US$561 (Rest of World), €366 (Europe), £2890 (UK). Prices are exc
sive of tax. Asia-Pacific GST, Canadian GST/HST and European VAT will be applied at the appropriate rates. For more information
current tax rates, please go to www.wileyonlinelibrary.com/tax-vat. The price includes online access to the current and all online bac
files to January 1st 2013, where available. For other pricing options, including access information and terms and conditions, please v
www.wileyonlinelibrary.com/access.

Delivery Terms and Legal Title

Where the subscription price includes print issues and delivery is to the recipient's address, delivery terms are **Delivered at Place (DA**
the recipient is responsible for paying any import duty or taxes. Title to all issues transfers FOB our shipping point, freight prepaid. We w
endeavour to fulfil claims for missing or damaged copies within six months of publication, within our reasonable discretion and subject
availability.

Back issues: Single issues from current and recent volumes are available at the current single issue price from cs-journals@wiley.com.

Disclaimer

The Publisher and Editors cannot be held responsible for errors or any consequences arising from the use of information contained in t
journal; the views and opinions expressed do not necessarily reflect those of the Publisher and Editors, neither does the publication
advertisements constitute any endorsement by the Publisher and Editors of the products advertised.

Publisher: *NEW DIRECTIONS FOR INSTITUTIONAL RESEARCH* is published by Wiley Periodicals, Inc., 350 Main St., Malden, MA 0214
5020.

Journal Customer Services: For ordering information, claims and any enquiry concerning your journal subscription please go
www.wileycustomerhelp.com/ask or contact your nearest office.
Americas: Email: cs-journals@wiley.com; Tel: +1 781 388 8598 or +1 800 835 6770 (toll free in the USA & Canada).
Europe, Middle East and Africa: Email: cs-journals@wiley.com; Tel: +44 (0) 1865 778315.
Asia Pacific: Email: cs-journals@wiley.com; Tel: +65 6511 8000.
Japan: For Japanese speaking support, Email: cs-japan@wiley.com.
Visit our Online Customer Help available in 7 languages at www.wileycustomerhelp.com/ask

Production Editor: Abha Mehta (email: abmehta@wiley.com).

Wiley's Corporate Citizenship initiative seeks to address the environmental, social, economic, and ethical challenges faced in our busi
ness and which are important to our diverse stakeholder groups. Since launching the initiative, we have focused on sharing our conte
with those in need, enhancing community philanthropy, reducing our carbon impact, creating global guidelines and best practices for p
per use, establishing a vendor code of ethics, and engaging our colleagues and other stakeholders in our efforts. Follow our progress
www.wiley.com/go/citizenship

View this journal online at wileyonlinelibrary.com/journal/ir

Wiley is a founding member of the UN-backed HINARI, AGORA, and OARE initiatives. They are now collectively known as Research4Lif
making online scientific content available free or at nominal cost to researchers in developing countries. Please visit Wiley's Content Acce
- Corporate Citizenship site: http://www.wiley.com/WileyCDA/Section/id-390082.html

Printed in the USA by The Sheridan Group.

Address for Editorial Correspondence: Editor-in chief, Gloria Crisp, *NEW DIRECTIONS FOR INSTITUTIONAL RESEARCH*, Emai
gloria.crisp@oregonstate.edu

Abstracting and Indexing Services

The Journal is indexed by Academic Search (EBSCO Publishing); Academic Search Alumni Edition (EBSCO Publishing); Academic Searc
Elite (EBSCO Publishing); Academic Search Premier (EBSCO Publishing); ERA: Educational Research Abstracts Online (T&F); ERIC
Educational Resources Information Center (CSC); Higher Education Abstracts (Claremont Graduate University); Professional Developmen
Collection (EBSCO Publishing).

Cover design: Wiley
Cover Images: © Lava 4 images | Shutterstock

For submission instructions, subscription and all other information visit:
wileyonlinelibrary.com/journal/ir

This issue is dedicated to the memory of NDIR Editor, Dr. John Ryan.

THE ASSOCIATION FOR INSTITUTIONAL RESEARCH (AIR) is the world's largest professional association for institutional researchers. The organization provides educational resources, best practices, and professional development opportunities for more than 4,000 members. Its primary purpose is to support members in the process of collecting, analyzing, and converting data into information that supports decision-making in higher education.

CONTENTS

EDITORS' NOTES

In 2016, the Association for Institutional Research (AIR) released its *Statement of Aspirational Practice for Institutional Research* (Swing & Ross, 2016a, 2016b). The *Statement* represents the efforts of the institution (AIR) to respond to the changing needs of postsecondary institutions. Its creation involved more than a year-long process and included an open call for ideas, crafting by six "subject matter experts" (2016b, p. 7), pilot testing at 10 institutions who vetted the statement, and feedback from more than 260 researchers (2016b). The statement release emphasized that some of its elements already exist at many institutions of higher education, but also recognized that much of what is included in the statement remains aspirational for most institutions (2016b).

The *Statement* suggests a new model of institutional research that moves it away from being the "one source of truth" (2016a, p. 2) and instead incorporates other institutional agents (i.e., students, faculty, and staff) not just as consumers or potential data sources, but also as institutional stewards and decision-makers in their own right. This is an important shift, with institutional research no longer confined to a service unit or office, but rather coaching and interacting with multiple decision makers. Importantly, the *Statement* proposes a student-focused paradigm, that is, one aimed at improving the student experience by "**intentionally** grounding institutional research initiatives and reports in a student-focused perspective" (2016b, p. 6, bold in original).

In this volume, we propose that one way to move institutional research (and researchers) toward the aspirational practices presented in the *Statement* is by more systematically incorporating qualitative research. We posit that qualitative research techniques can add depth to current institutional research practices and promote a holistic understanding of student experiences. Our work is anchored by Terenzini's (1993) definition of institutional research as a form of organizational intelligence and discussion of the various awarenesses required to cultivate organizational intelligence. Terenzini (1993) described organizational intelligence as arising from technical/analytical awareness, issues awareness, and contextual awareness. The technical/analytical domain of organizational intelligence consists of having the requisite methodological skills to construct a systematic research design and execute it with rigor and probity. Issues awareness is based on the ability of the institutional researcher to identify pressing organizational problems and to generate information that can help facilitate decision

NEW DIRECTIONS FOR INSTITUTIONAL RESEARCH, no. 174 © 2017 Wiley Periodicals, Inc.
Published online in Wiley Online Library (wileyonlinelibrary.com) • DOI: 10.1002/ir.20216

making related to them. Finally, knowledge of context focuses on the way in which these individual problems fit into the broader complex systems in the institution and the broader ecologies of which the institution is a part.

Individually and collectively the chapters in this volume present the argument that qualitative research can serve as a mechanism to produce organizational intelligence. They also hint at how very difficult it may be to achieve true organizational intelligence without at least some use of qualitative research. Although institutional researchers often employ informal qualitative methods (their experiences and anecdotal observations) to anchor their understandings of issues and context, we argue that the creation of true organizational intelligence is facilitated by formalizing the qualitative data collection and analysis process in institutional research. To that end, we present a systematic approach to qualitative research in institutional research that connects technical and analytical skills with issues awareness and knowledge of context. As a result, we organized the volume following Terenzini's (1993) definition of organizational intelligence. Chapters 1 and 2 describe technical/analytical awareness practices, Chapters 3 and 4 are dedicated to issues awareness, and Chapters 5 and 6 present practices that achieve contextual awareness.

In Chapter 1 ("A Qualitative Toolkit for Institutional Research"), Chrystal A. George Mwangi and Genia M. Bettencourt provide tools, resources, and examples for effectively grounding and conducting qualitative inquiry as a part of institutional research and assessment. The authors provide a review of key qualitative skills and knowledge areas, focusing on research paradigms, specific methodologies and methods, and data analysis. This chapter presents concrete ways for institutional researchers to build qualitative research competencies and to support the development of organizational intelligence in institutional research and assessment through the use of qualitative inquiry among its professionals. In Chapter 2 ("Integrity Is More Than Validity: Seeking Credible, Usable, and Ethical Research"), Sharon F. Rallis and Rachael B. Lawrence present a use-centered understanding of validity that is anchored in practical and responsive use of data. Together, these chapters illustrate practical ways to use qualitative research to enrich common technical and analytical awareness practices in institutional research through the use of alternative epistemological, methodological, and analytic frameworks.

In Chapter 3 ("Using Mixed Methods to Assess Initiatives with Broad-Based Goals"), Karen Kurotsuchi Inkelas describes an innovative, mixed-methods assessment design that can be used to provide evidence of an initiative's effectiveness in changing behaviors, and to inform decision-making for future programming needs. She presents a teaching and pedagogy workshop to exemplify how this type of assessment can yield not only summative but also formative data to inform decision-making. Using examples drawn from a qualitative study of belonging among students with disabilities, Rachel E. Friedensen, Byron P. McCrae, and Ezekiel Kimball demonstrate in Chapter 4 ("Using Qualitative Research to Document Variations in Student Experience") how qualitative evidence can add depth to quantitative information about what is generally true of all students while also complicating that messaging by describing differences in experiences for a specific group of students. These two chapters exemplify issues-awareness types of organizational intelligence through the use of qualitative data to include and inform multiple institutional decision-makers.

Chapters 5 and 6 provide examples of qualitative practices that reach contextual awareness in institutional research projects that use a qualitative research approach (the case study). Elizabeth A. Williams and Martha L.A. Stassen present a case study describing their three-pronged approach integrating information derived from qualitative inquiry into planning and assessment cycles typically dominated by quantitative information in Chapter 5 ("Context Matters: Using Qualitative Inquiry to Inform Departmental Effectiveness and Student Success"). Using their qualitative inquiry cycle as a guide, the authors describe the creation of contextual awareness as an integral part of effective institutional research work. In Chapter 6 ("Cooperative Attention: Using Qualitative Case Studies to Study Peer Institutions"), Bethany Lisi uses the metaphor of the divided brain to describe the difficult work of promoting contextual awareness as a part of organizational intelligence and to demonstrate the importance of case studies in its cultivation. Lisi uses the analogy of cooperative attention of the two sides of a brain that must work cooperatively to describe both the interplay between technical, issues, and contextual intelligence, as well as the need for institutional researchers to activate both levels of attention—narrow focus on institutional issues and broad awareness of contextual patterns—to maintain organizational intelligence.

In the concluding Chapter 7 ("Using Qualitative Inquiry to Promote Organizational Intelligence"), we (the editors) integrate the arguments and examples deployed throughout the volume into a coherent call for action for institutional and educational researchers to rethink their work and practice to respond to the changing needs of higher education institutions. This chapter illustrates the importance of qualitative research in institutional research practices that respond to the aspirational practices captured in the Statement. This is possible for at least two reasons: First, qualitative research can help institutional researchers capture, include, and communicate the voices, perspectives, and needs of different institutional agents in colleges and universities. Second, qualitative research, framed under Terenzini's (1993) view of institutional research as organizational intelligence, can support the efforts of institutional researchers to gain the knowledge and skills required to push beyond technical/analytical intelligence (first tier) and toward issues (second tier) and contextual (third tier) intelligences.

Karla I. Loya
Ezekiel Kimball
Editors

References

Swing, R. L., & Ross, L. E. (2016a). A new vision for institutional research. *Change: The Magazine of Higher Learning, 48*(2), 6–13.

Swing, R. L., & Ross, L. E. (2016b). *Statement of aspirational practice for institutional research* (pp. 1–11). Tallahassee, FL: Association for Institutional Research. Retrieved from https://www.airweb.org/aspirationalstatement

Terenzini, P. T. (1993). On the nature of institutional research and skills if requires. *Research in Higher Education, 34*(1), 1–10.

KARLA I. LOYA *is an assistant professor of educational leadership at the University of Hartford.*

EZEKIEL KIMBALL *is an assistant professor of higher education at the University of Massachusetts Amherst.*

NEW DIRECTIONS FOR INSTITUTIONAL RESEARCH • DOI: 10.1002/ir

1

This chapter provides tools, resources, and examples for engaging qualitative inquiry as a part of institutional research and assessment. It supports the development of individual ability and organizational intelligence in qualitative inquiry.

A Qualitative Toolkit for Institutional Research

Chrystal A. George Mwangi, Genia M. Bettencourt

As an institutional researcher, Sam has just finished analyzing the results of their institutions' most recent campus climate study. The quantitative findings show clearly that Students of Color have negative experiences both within academic courses and co-curricular involvement. Students of Color responded in high numbers to questions about microaggressions on campus, indicating that these pervasive acts of racism permeate their daily experiences. Students of Color were also more likely to report feeling isolation on campus and dissatisfaction with the institution. Sam wants to know more about microaggressions on campus to be able to understand their different manifestations, the impact they have on Students of Color, and potential strategies for intervention. To meet these goals, Sam decides to conduct qualitative research centered on the voices of these students experiencing microaggressions.

Qualitative research is the result of many different decisions, all of which are made within unique contexts. To illustrate these decisions and contexts, we use the example of Sam throughout this chapter. Like Sam, many institutional researchers find they need to integrate traditionally quantitative approaches with qualitative methodologies to obtain the full picture of student experiences in higher education. Qualitative methods naturally align with institutional inquiry that focuses on students' experiences within a certain context or set of conditions (Harper & Kuh, 2007). As institutions engage in increasingly complex data-driven decision-making, "the best decisions are based on a deeper understanding than quantitative methods alone can provide" (Van Note Chism & Banta, 2007, p. 15). As such, it is crucial for institutional researchers and institutional research offices to develop qualitative expertise to support methodologies and methods that can be applied to a spectrum of research questions (McLaughlin, McLaughlin, & Muffo, 2001). This chapter provides tools, resources, and

NEW DIRECTIONS FOR INSTITUTIONAL RESEARCH, no. 174 © 2017 Wiley Periodicals, Inc.
Published online in Wiley Online Library (wileyonlinelibrary.com) • DOI: 10.1002/ir.20217

11

examples for effectively grounding and conducting qualitative inquiry as a part of institutional research and assessment. We review key qualitative skills and knowledge areas such as research paradigms, methodologies, and methods.

Paradigms

Paradigms, also known as worldviews, are "systems of beliefs and practices that influence how researchers select both the questions they study and methods that they use to study them" (Morgan, 2007, p. 50). All types of research are rooted in researchers' paradigms. Paradigms emerge out of researchers' epistemology, ontology, and axiology, shaping how knowledge is sought out and interpreted. These approaches shape the choices a researcher makes in what and how to pursue their topic.

Although there are multiple classifications of paradigms, for simplicity, we utilize four overarching categories (Creswell, 2014; Mertens, 2015):

The positivist paradigm focuses on explaining, testing, and predicting phenomena (Guido, Chávez, & Lincoln, 2010). Information is objective and value-free, and exists within one true reality. This paradigm has evolved into postpositivism by incorporating a more critical lens to examine how a cause determines an effect or outcome (Creswell, 2014). In the former, a researcher might conduct a study to prove a hypothesis is correct and to discover the truth. In the latter, researchers aim to reject a null (false) hypothesis to move closer to the truth.

The constructivist, or interpretive, paradigm views knowledge as socially constructed and individuals' experiences as framed by their unique context. Individuals have a subjective reality based on understanding their views (Creswell, 2014). Instead of a universal Truth, there are only truths that exist for individuals that are reliant on their context and time (Guido et al., 2010).

The critical, or transformative, paradigm can incorporate numerous theories that examine the experiences of marginalized individuals and unequal distributions of power. This approach tends to emphasize collaborative research processes to avoid perpetuating power imbalances (Creswell, 2014). These approaches look to restructure the status quo, with the goal of social change. Critical designs may utilize nonhierarchical methodologies that aim to involve participants as co-researchers on investigating a problem and implementing change, such as participatory action research. More widely, critical researchers also cite this paradigm as a way of interpreting results.

The pragmatic paradigm emphasizes that researchers choose the methods, processes, and tools that best answer the research question at hand (Creswell, 2014). Pragmatic paradigms are most commonly associated with mixed-methods research.

NEW DIRECTIONS FOR INSTITUTIONAL RESEARCH • DOI: 10.1002/ir

Sam is interested in engaging in-depth with student voices and experiences, to understand how their experiences on campus are informed by their interactions with others, their daily lives, and their social identities. As such, Sam identifies that their research is rooted in a constructivist paradigm that prioritizes the context of diverse groups of students to learn more about their experiences and perspectives.

Crafting Questions

Qualitative data can provide a great deal of information, some of which may be beyond the scope and nature of what the researcher wants to investigate. Like research paradigms, crafting a research question(s) helps to constrain the scope of a study. Research questions provide guidance for one's inquiry and require a response that emerges from data and analysis. When a study becomes overwhelming, it is important to remember that a primary goal is to answer the research question(s). Good research questions stem from the purpose of the study. Consider whether the research purpose is to describe a phenomenon or explain and theorize about it (Marshall & Rossman, 2006). Is it to explore a problem that has not been previously examined or to empower others and create greater equity (Marshall & Rossman, 2006)? Answering these can help determine how to craft the research question(s). The methodology is another way to help develop the research question(s). For example, an ethnographic study often incorporates a question about culture. Similarly, a theoretical/conceptual framework may also influence the nature of the question(s).

Qualitative research questions are distinct from quantitative research questions in that they tend to ask: How? and/or What? Qualitative research questions often do not begin with "Why?" because this tends to be driven by cause and effect or a quantitative purpose. It is important that qualitative research questions cannot be answered with a simple yes, no, or one-word discrete answer. They should balance breadth and specificity. For example, a researcher may want to ask a question that will solve a major problem on campus. However, given the complexity of that problem, the study may not be able to solve it. Instead, ask questions that engage the larger problem by contributing to its solution or that contribute to a better understanding of the problem. The question(s) should be feasible and researchable given one's resources, skills, and knowledge (Lawrence-Lightfoot, 2016). As with other parts of qualitative inquiry, the development of a research question can also be an iterative process. In fact, Stage and Manning (2016) state, "Rarely is a research question as clear in the beginning of the study as it is at the end" (p. 8). Therefore, researchers can change or revise the research question (or add subquestions) as the study progresses and the data emerge. Sam asks two research questions:

1. How do Students of Color experience microaggressions on campus?

2. What impact do Students of Color perceive microaggressions have on their college experience?

The first question allows for the collection of data that describes occurrences of microaggressions toward Students of Color and focuses on these students' lived experience. Although qualitative data cannot produce "cause and effect" findings, they can elucidate the perceived impact of an action. The second question will lead Sam to collect data that describes the way that Students of Color feel affected by microaggressions to demonstrate the severity of the problem and inform campus interventions.

Overview of Methodologies

Methodologies demonstrate branches of knowledge and strategies of inquiry that influence research choices (Patton, 2015). They are the guideposts that help a researcher ground a study and shape additional components of the research design. Although some studies claim a generic qualitative approach without selecting a methodology, thinking systematically about methodology can help researchers to align research questions, data collection processes, and data analyses (Patton, 2015). There are many different qualitative methodologies, but here we have selected four of the more common in higher education research: case study, ethnography, grounded theory, and narrative inquiry.

Case Study.   Case study is an appropriate method when the researcher wants to explore contextual conditions that might be critical to the phenomenon of study (Yin, 2003). Within this approach, it is essential to define the boundaries of a case, which are set in terms of time, place, events, and/or processes (Merriam, 1998; Yin, 2003). The case (also described as a bounded system or unit of analysis) is the focus of the study (Merriam, 2009). Case study researchers utilize several sources of information in data collection to provide in-depth description and explanation of the case (Merriam, 2009). Research can be comprised of a single case or multiple cases that are analyzed and/or compared. There are different types of case studies. For example, a descriptive case study generates a rich, thick, and detailed account that conveys understanding and explanation of a phenomenon (Merriam, 1998). Interpretive case studies go beyond describing the phenomena to present data that support, challenge, or expand existing theories (Merriam, 2009). Finally, exploratory case studies help to determine the feasibility of a research project and solidify research questions and processes (Yin, 2003).

Ethnography.   Situated within the field of anthropology, ethnographers seek to understand and describe cultural and/or social groups (Spradley, 1979). Ethnographic studies examine individuals and groups interacting in ordinary settings and attempt to discern pervasive patterns such as life cycles, events, and cultural themes. Ethnography describes a culture-sharing group, uses themes or perspectives of the culture-sharing group for organizational analysis, and seeks interpretation of the culture-sharing group for meanings of social interaction (Spradley, 1979). Ethnography assumes that the principal research interest is largely affected by community cultural understandings. Thus, "ethnographies recreate for the reader the shared beliefs, practices, artifacts, folk knowledge, and behaviors of some group of people" (LeCompte, Preissle, & Tesch, 1993, pp. 2–3). Ethnography can be emic (focused on the perspectives of the group under study), etic (focused on the researcher/outsider perspective), or blend the two approaches. The ethnographic process of inquiry suggests prolonged observation within a natural setting and in-depth interviews. Ethnographic studies also define the researcher as a key instrument in the data collection process, who describes and interprets observations of the cultural group (Mertens, 2015).

Grounded Theory.   Grounded theory is an explanatory methodology developed to construct theory that emerges from and is grounded in data (Glaser & Strauss, 1967). Through this process, researchers can create a substantive theory, which is a working theory for a specific social process or context (Corbin & Strauss, 2008; Strauss & Corbin, 1998; Glaser & Strauss, 1967). Grounded theorists do not use theoretical frameworks and historically have sought to limit a priori knowledge of the problem being studied (Glaser & Strauss, 1967), but more recent approaches have emphasized the need for sensitizing concepts, or ideas from extant literature, to provide a structure for inquiry (Charmaz, 2014). This allows for substantive theory to be created inductively, from the data. Grounded theory is also defined by its sampling and data analysis procedures. Grounded theory researchers use theoretical sampling by selecting participants based on relevant constructs and participants' experience with the phenomenon under study, rather than solely demographic criteria (Strauss & Corbin, 1998). Researchers should use data from their initial sample as a guide for recruiting additional participants to provide data to address emerging categories (Charmaz, 2014; Corbin & Strauss, 2008; Strauss & Corbin, 1998). When new data from the sample no longer add to a category or concept, the study has reached theoretical saturation and the sampling process ends. Grounded theory is also known for the constant comparative method of analysis in which data are iteratively collected and compared to emerging categories through a coding process (Strauss & Corbin, 1998). The constant comparative method will be further explained in the Data Analysis section.

Narrative Inquiry.   Narrative inquiry centers on telling a story or stories and thus "takes as its object of investigation the story itself" (Riessman, 1993, p. 1). Researchers using this methodology organize the narrative of a single participant or narratives of multiple participants to share, shape, and connect their experiences (Chase, 2011). Chronology and timeline are central features of narrative inquiry (although narratives themselves do not need to follow a linear story). In addition, this methodological approach often involves multiple, in-depth interviews and/or other data such as existing documents, and necessitates a reflexive relationship between researchers and their participants in order to re-tell stories through empirical findings (Chase, 2011). Data collection methods for this approach should allow for telling by the participant(s), interpretation of the experience(s) by the researcher, representation of the story or stories, and reflection on assumptions made about the self while engaging in telling and re-telling the narratives (Jackson & Mazzei, 2013). There are many forms of narrative inquiry, including oral histories, biographies, testimonies, and memoirs. Given Sam's interest in focusing on the voices of Students of Color regarding microaggressions, they select narrative inquiry. This methodology can use participants' stories to expose oppressive actions (Chase, 2011). Narrative inquiry will shape the study's emphasis on examining students' experiences with microaggressions throughout their time at the university and in eliciting specific examples or stories, related to those experiences.

Tools for Data Collection

The main types of data collection in qualitative research include participant observation, individual interviews, and focus groups (Guest, Namey, & Mitchell, 2013). The research questions and methodologies may lead toward a certain type of data collection, or a study that combines multiple approaches to gather data (multimodal design). All three approaches require some initial planning beyond crafting questions to include establishing a location, obtaining any necessary tools prior to implementation (e.g., recording devices), and dedicating time immediately afterward to process through initial reflections and analysis (Guest et al., 2013).

Observations. Observations are typically the result of the researcher's experiences in a given situation or environment. As opposed to direct observation, like the detail recovered by a video camera or a two-way mirror, participant observation includes the researcher as a part of the environment directly absorbing and processing information (Guest et al., 2013). Researchers are engaged in the environment by taking notes, recording their environment, and asking questions to uncover meaning (Guest et al., 2013). This form of data collection is used to discover complex interactions in social settings (Marshall & Rossman, 2006). By being in a space where the topic of interest occurs, researchers record the behavior of interest as it happens and to provide context (Merriam, 2009). The degree of what a researcher can observe may be determined by the relationships they have in the community, the access they negotiate, and the amount of time spent gathering data (Guest et al., 2013).

In observations, the goal of the researcher is to record field notes with a high degree of detail. These notes involve physical surroundings, context, people, and their actions (Neuman, 2006). Prior to beginning observations, the researcher should choose an organizational system that will allow for tracking direct observations with inferences, analysis, and personal journaling (Neuman, 2006). Although many of these notes are conducted during the observation, the researcher should also budget time shortly after finishing the observation to jot down additional notes. The time after observation may be used to create analytic memos in which to record plans, reflect on ethical decisions, and create maps or diagrams of occurrences or relationships (Neuman, 2006). Although observations may involve a large time commitment of many hours, as a form of data collection they allow for a researcher to engage directly with human behavior, particularly of which participants are less aware or able to discuss.

Interviews.   The most popular form of data collection, individual interviews use open-ended questions to learn about participants' experiences, memories, reflections, and opinions (Magnusson & Marecek, 2015). Different types of interviews allow researchers to incorporate varying degrees of flexibility as desired by their paradigm, methodology, and style. There are four interview types (Rossman and Rallis 2017; adapted from Patton, 2015): (a) informal interviews in a casual setting, often recorded through field notes; (b) a guided interview guide approach, with preset categories and topics but flexibility to address emerging topics; (c) a standardized open-ended interview with a set order of fixed questions; and (d) true conversations in the form of dialogic interviews. The goal of an interview is to gain rich, in-depth, personal experiences that relate directly to the research topic (Magnusson & Marecek, 2015).

To conduct an interview, a researcher should have "superb listening skills and be skillful at personal interaction, question framing, and gentle probing for elaboration" (Marshall & Rossman, 2006). Guest and colleagues (2013) recommend using interviews to gain in-depth insight, explore new topics, and gain information about potentially sensitive or polarizing topics. In approaching interviews, they provide the following suggestions:

Schedule interviews at times that are mutually convenient, with an emphasis on the interviewee's preferences
Allot around 45–90 minutes for an in-depth interview
Pilot the interview protocol prior to implementation to ensure effectiveness
Plan ahead for what kind of data will be needed during analysis. This can include summaries of the conversation, expanded interview notes, audio/video recordings, and verbatim transcripts.

Although these suggestions provide an initial framework, all decisions around interviews are contingent on an understanding of the participants and topic under study.

Focus Groups.   For researchers interested in understanding how individuals discuss a topic collectively, focus groups can save time and money while gathering rich data. Focus groups tend to be most useful to gain information on group norms and processes, opinions and perspectives, reactions and responses, and brainstorming (Guest et al., 2013). Because focus groups allow the researcher to see real-time responses, they provide beneficial opportunities to view how individuals agree, disagree, or respond to one another. A key benefit of focus groups is their assumption that an individual's attitudes and beliefs do not form in a vacuum; participants develop their opinions and understandings by engaging with others (Marshall & Rossman, 2006).

The ideal group contains approximately 7–10 individuals that are ideally strangers, to encourage varying viewpoints (Rossman & Rallis, 2017). Utilizing strangers also helps to decrease social desirability bias that can occur in interview settings to respond or behave in a certain way. Depending on the study, researchers could choose to recruit homogenous or heterogeneous groups of participants (Mertens, 2015). As focus groups include multiple moving pieces, they rely greatly on the skill of the facilitator to keep the conversation on track, ask appropriate probes, and ensure a balance of voices. Interview protocols should establish ground rules prior to beginning, prioritize key questions to allow for as much fluidity in the conversation as possible, and create a limited time commitment (Guest et al., 2013).

For their study, Sam decides to do individual interviews to understand how Students of Color describe microaggressions and their manifestations within the context of their overall college experience. Sam chooses interviews because microaggressions can be a sensitive topic for individuals to share in a focus group, and there is no clear context in which Sam could conduct observations of this behavior. They choose a standardized open-ended interview with questions that include

1. In thinking about the past week, can you describe any microaggressions you have encountered and the context in which they occurred?
2. How would you describe the impact of these microaggressions on your overall student experience?

Sam prepares prompts for the interview questions and pilots the interview protocol with several colleagues who identify as People of Color before determining that the interviews will last around an hour each.

Data Analysis

Although there are numerous qualitative data analysis techniques, they all share at least three common characteristics. First, the qualitative data analysis process often begins during data collection. Thus, the analytic process is considered iterative or non linear (Creswell, 2014). A researcher may collect data and engage in early analysis only to realize that more data are needed to understand the participants' experiences. Even when formal data analysis does not begin while data collection is ongoing, qualitative researchers often use memos to document emerging ideas and patterns, which form the basis for subsequent analysis. Initial data analysis that occurs during data collection can also allow researchers to consider whether they are obtaining the type and quality of information they intended. Second, a major goal of qualitative data analysis is data reduction (Creswell, 2014). Qualitative research can produce large amounts of data and the analytic process works to reduce the volume of information by identifying major patterns and themes within it. Researchers can engage this process on their own, in teams, and/or using computer-assisted qualitative data analysis software (CAQDA) such as NVIVO (see Bazeley & Jackson, 2013) or Atlas.ti. Third, the process is immersive, meaning that it requires a high level of engagement with the data. This can include reading and rereading interview transcripts multiple times to exhaust exploration of the data. During this process, researchers often write memos that help to document initial interpretations of the data as well as engage in reflexivity (e.g., processing how one's background, biases, and perspectives may influence the analytic process) (Lincoln & Guba, 1985). These memos can be used as part of one's audit trail, which is a record of research steps that helps to ensure data quality and transparency (Lincoln & Guba, 1985).

One popular analytical tool is the constant comparative method. Although grounded theorists developed this method, it is commonly used as a general tool for analyzing data and is useful for those learning how to engage in qualitative analysis because it provides a specific three-phase process. This process is known as coding, in which short words or phrases are used to "assign a summative, salient, essence-capturing, and/or evocative attribute for a portion of language-based or visual data" (Saldaña, 2013, p. 3). Codes can reflect activities, relationships, roles, processes, emotions, perspectives, and other units of social organization. The constant comparative method begins with open coding words, lines, several sentences, or paragraphs of data. Open coding can be deductive and/or inductive (Strauss & Corbin, 1998). Deductive codes stem from borrowed concepts such as components of the theoretical framework or key themes from relevant literature. Inductive or in vivo codes are emergent from the data. Inductive coding can be developed from data that "strike as interesting, potentially relevant, or important to the study . . . for answering the research questions" (Merriam, 2009, p. 178). Whether the open codes are deductive or inductive, it is important to identify the codes with names and definitions clearly (Miles & Huberman, 2005).

The next stage in the constant comparative method is axial coding, which is performed iteratively during the open coding process and also after open codes are developed. This stage begins the reduction process and includes comparing and connecting emerging codes into categories (Strauss & Corbin, 1998). Categories are "conceptual elements that cover or span many individual examples or codes previously identified" (Merriam, 2009, p. 181). For example, while a researcher may have 100 open codes, the researcher might reduce these codes into 20 categories. One can do this by grouping together data by related open codes to reassemble the data and demonstrate recurrent patterns and themes (Strauss & Corbin, 1998). The axial coding process is also useful for separating data that are essential to the purpose of the study from data that fall outside the scope of the research purpose and question(s). The final phase of the constant comparative approach is selective coding; however, some researchers will only perform open and axial coding, particularly for exploratory studies. During the selective coding process, the researcher pulls together themes to develop a storyline and identify a core category (Strauss & Corbin, 1998). The core category "is the central defining aspect of the phenomenon to which all other categories and hypotheses are related or interconnect" (Merriam, 2009, p. 200). For example, moving from 20 categories to potentially one to five overarching themes. This reflects the primary narrative emerging across the data that provides a response to the research question(s).

Sam considers the constant comparative approach, but instead chooses an analytic approach that stems from narrative inquiry. This involves four phases: (a) initial reading of transcripts to indicate general themes and consider how each part contributes to the whole story; (b) rereading the transcripts to view whether there are multiple narratives present and to consider the structure, content, and larger contexts involved; (c) investigate the patterns emerging which includes how the whole story and its parts are told; and (d) engage the literature/theoretical framework with the participants' narrative(s) to glean a more in-depth understanding of the story (Josselson, 2011).

Research Quality

Although quantitative inquiry strives for reliability and validity, in qualitative research, trustworthiness is the predominant standard of research quality (Guba & Lincoln, 1989; Lincoln & Guba, 1985). Trustworthiness can be established in multiple ways. One is by producing work that is transferable, or that provides enough context for readers to infer similar results in their own context (Krefting, 1999; Lincoln & Guba, 1985). This can be done by providing detailed documentation of data collection and analysis procedures as well as by using thick, rich description of participants' experiences (Krefting, 1999; Lincoln & Guba, 1985). One goal of qualitative research is credibility or having data that accurately reflects the phenomenon (Krefting, 1999; Lincoln & Guba, 1985). Fostering credibility can begin during the data collection phase with prolonged engagement with participants.

Another tool is member checking, which involves testing the interpretations of the data with study participants by sharing initial data analysis for their feedback (Krefting, 1999; Lincoln & Guba, 1985). Peer debriefing requires meeting with an individual who is unaffiliated with the research (disinterested peers) and can give honest feedback (equal power dynamic) about the plausibility of data interpretations. Additionally, triangulation can be built into the research design to produce divergent constructions of reality (Lincoln & Guba, 1985). For example, one can engage methodological triangulation through use of multiple forms of data collection (interviews, participant observation) or data triangulation through multiple data sources. Triangulation can also be performed through the involvement of multiple researchers or analyst triangulation) or during data analysis through the use of multiple theoretical frames (theory/perspective triangulation) (Patton, 2015). Triangulation can establish confirmability to ensure that findings are shaped more by study participants than by researcher biases. Reflexive processes such as journaling, engaging in dialogue with other researchers, and naming one's positionality (e.g., relationship between researcher and participants/study topic) within the write-up of the study can develop confirmability. Lastly, trustworthy studies should be dependable, or demonstrate consistent findings that could be repeated (Lincoln & Guba 1985). To establish dependability (and confirmability), researchers can create an audit trail that documents the steps and processes they engaged in during the qualitative investigation.

Sam selects multiple strategies to increase the trustworthiness of the study. One is member checking. Sam sends each of the participants their transcript with initial interpretations and questions. After giving the participant time to review the transcript and notes, Sam calls each participant to briefly ensure that the interpretations reflect the participants' meaning and to clarify any questions about the narratives. Another is by using thick, rich description by including direct quotes from participants in the final write-up of the study. Lastly, Sam engages in peer debriefing with an institutional researcher in the office. This individual is not involved in the study, but is a Person of Color who graduated from a predominantly white institution 3 years prior.

Conclusion

Qualitative research provides an important opportunity to engage with participants' experiences through their own voices and behaviors. Unlike quantitative methodologies, qualitative approaches view the researcher as the instrument through which data are collected (Patton, 2015). As such, intentional engagement throughout each step of the research process is crucial to ensure a well-aligned, accurate, and ethical design. Successful use of qualitative methodologies fosters opportunities for institutional researchers to pursue new questions and experiences within their work (McLaughlin et al., 2001). The rest of the volume continues to look at specific contexts and considerations in which qualitative research can aid institutional research.

References

Bazeley, P., & Jackson, K. (2013). *Qualitative data analysis with NVIVO.* Thousand Oaks, CA: Sage.

Charmaz, K. (2014). *Constructing grounded theory* (2nd ed.). Thousand Oaks, CA: Sage.

Chase, S. E. (2011). Narrative inquiry: Still a field in the making. In N. K. Denzin & Y. S. Lincoln (Eds.), *The Sage handbook of qualitative research* (4th ed., pp. 421–434). Thousand Oaks, CA: Sage.

Corbin, J., & Strauss, A. (2008). *The basics of qualitative research: Techniques and procedures for developing grounded theory.* Thousand Oaks, CA: Sage.

Creswell, J. W. (2014). *Research design: Qualitative, quantitative, and mixed approaches* (4th ed.). Thousand Oaks, CA: Sage.

Glaser, B. G., & Strauss, A. L. (1967). *The discovery of grounded theory: Strategies for qualitative research.* New York, NY: Aldine.

Guba, E. G., & Lincoln, Y. S. (1989). *Fourth-generation evaluation.* Newbury Park, CA: Sage.

Guest, G., Namey, E. M., & Mitchell, M. L. (2013). *Collecting qualitative data: A field manual for applied research.* Thousand Oaks, CA: Sage.

Guido, F. M., Chávez, A. F., & Lincoln, Y. S. (2010). Underlying paradigms in student affairs research and practice. *Journal of Student Affairs Research and Practice, 47*(1), 1–22. https://doi.org/10.2202/1949-6605.66017

Harper, S. R., & Kuh, G. D. (2007). Myths and misconceptions about using qualitative methods in assessment. *New Directions for Institutional Research, 136,* 5–14. https://doi.org/10.1002/ir.227

Jackson, A., & Mazzei, L. (2013). Plugging one text into another: Thinking with theory in qualitative research. *Qualitative Inquiry, 19*(4), 261–271.

Josselson, R. (2011). Narrative research: Constructing, deconstructing, and reconstructing story. In F. J. Wertz, K. Charmaz, L. M. McMullen, R. Josselson, R. Anderson, & E. McSpadden (Eds.), *Five ways of doing qualitative analysis: Phenomenological psychology, grounded theory, discourse analysis, narrative research, and intuitive inquiry* (pp. 224–242). New York, NY: The Guilford Press.

Krefting, L. (1999). Rigor in qualitative research: The assessment of trustworthiness. In A. Miliniki (Ed.), *Cases in qualitative research: Research reports for discussion and evaluation* (pp. 173–181). Los Angeles, CA: Puscale.

Lawrence-Lightfoot, S. (2016). Portraiture methodology: Blending art and science. *Learning Landscapes, 9*(2), 19–27.

LeCompte, M. D., Preissle, J., & Tesch, R. (1993) *Ethnography and qualitative design in educational research* (2nd ed.). San Diego, CA: Academic Press.

Lincoln, Y. S., & Guba, E. G. (1985). *Naturalistic inquiry.* Newbury Park, CA: Sage.

Magnusson, E., & Marecek, J. (2015). *Doing interview-based qualitative research: A learner's guide.* Cambridge, UK: Cambridge University Press.

Marshall, C., & Rossman, G. B. (2006). *Designing qualitative research* (4th ed.). Thousand Oaks, CA: Sage.

McLaughlin, J. S., McLaughlin, G. W., & Muffo, J. A. (2001). Using qualitative and quantitative methods for complementary purposes: A case study. *New Directions for Institutional Research, 112,* 15–44. https://doi.org/10.1002/ir.26

Merriam, S. B. (1998). *Qualitative research and case study applications in education.* San Francisco, CA: Jossey-Bass.

Merriam, S. B. (2009). *Qualitative research: A guide to design and implementation*. San Francisco, CA: Jossey-Bass.

Mertens, D. M. (2015). *Research and evaluation in education and psychology: Integrating Diversity with quantitative, qualitative, and mixed methods* (4th ed.). Los Angeles, CA: Sage.

Miles, M. B., & Huberman, A. M. (2005). *Qualitative data analysis*. Thousand Oaks, CA: Sage.

Morgan, D. L. (2007). Paradigms lost and pragmatism regained: Methodological implications of combining qualitative and quantitative methods. *Journal of Mixed Methods Research*, 1(1), 48–76. https://doi.org/10.1177/2345678906292462

Neuman, W. L. (2006). *Social research methods: Qualitative and quantitative approaches* (6th ed.). Boston, MA: Pearson.

Patton, M. Q. (2015). *Qualitative research & evaluation methods: Integrating theory and practice* (4th ed.). Thousand Oaks, CA: Sage.

Riessman, C. K. (1993). *Narrative analysis*. Newbury Park, CA: Sage.

Rossman, G. B., & Rallis, S. F. (2017). *An introduction to qualitative research: Learning in the field* (4th ed.). Los Angeles, CA: Sage.

Saldaña, J. (2013). *The coding manual for qualitative researchers* (2nd ed.). Thousand Oaks, CA: Sage.

Spradley, J. P. (1979). *The ethnographic interview*. New York, NY: Holt, Rinehart and Winston.

Stage, F. K., & Manning, K. (Eds.). (2016). *Research in the college context: Approaches and methods* (2nd ed.). New York, NY: Routledge.

Strauss, A., & Corbin, J. (1998). *Basics of qualitative research: Techniques and procedures for developing grounded theory*. Thousand Oaks, CA: Sage.

Van Note Chism, N., & Banta, T. W. (2007). Enhancing institutional assessment efforts through qualitative methods. *New Directions for Institutional Research*, 136, 15–28. https://doi.org/10.1002/ir.228

Yin, R. K. (2003). *Case study research: Design and methods* (3rd ed.). Thousand Oaks, CA: Sage.

CHRYSTAL A. GEORGE MWANGI *is an assistant professor of higher education at the University of Massachusetts Amherst.*

GENIA M. BETTENCOURT *is a doctoral candidate in higher education at the University of Massachusetts Amherst.*

2

This chapter introduces integrity and use as central concepts for judging research quality. Analyzing an illustrative case through the NRC Guiding Principles for Education Research and Terenzini's tiers of intelligence, we demonstrate the centrality of research integrity to use.

Integrity Is More Than Validity: Seeking Credible, Usable, and Ethical Research

Sharon F. Rallis, Rachael B. Lawrence

Organizational intelligence describes an inquiry process that emphasizes use. Terenzini (1993) proposes that three tiers of personal competence and institutional understanding—that is, intelligence—are required for use: technical/analytical, issues awareness, and contextual knowledge. Data are generated, analyzed, synthesized, and interpreted into information that becomes knowledge when used to inform institutional understanding and the decision-making that sets institutional direction. To be usable, the pieces of the research process must fit together, must be coherent. Each decision in the process must also be morally sound, balance potential benefit and harm, and treat participants with fairness and respect. Building on Terenzini's conceptualization of research, we suggest that it is this integrity of the research (both process and results) that determines its truth-value (validity) and usefulness.

Although much debated by qualitative researchers (e.g., Cho & Trent, 2006; Maxwell, 1992; Onwuegbuzie & Leech, 2007), validity has traditionally been the primary criterion for determining research quality or value in social sciences. Shadish, Cook, and Campbell (2002) define validity as "the truth of, correctness of, or degree of support for an inference" (p. 513). This definition focuses on establishing the legitimacy of the inferences and conclusions drawn from the data. However, this seemingly simple framing is not without potential challenges.

These challenges to validity stem from the subjective nature of truth. Philosophers and social scientists have shown that our understanding of truth is socially constructed and influenced by power, positionality, and context (e.g., Foucault & Blasius, 1993; Heshusius, 1994; Peshkin, 1988; Ratner, 2002). Additionally, because all data, whether qualitative

NEW DIRECTIONS FOR INSTITUTIONAL RESEARCH, no. 174 © 2017 Wiley Periodicals, Inc.
Published online in Wiley Online Library (wileyonlinelibrary.com) • DOI: 10.1002/ir.20218

or quantitative, stem from the theoretical and methodological decisions used to produce them, one might argue that "theories or methods create facts. And theories, in turn, are grounded in and derived from the basic philosophical assumptions their formulators hold regarding the nature of and functional relationship between the individual, society, and science" (Ratcliffe, 1983, p. 148). Thus, validity of inferences and conclusions relies on alignment with the worldview of the researcher who also serves to interpret—to use—the data. Although quantitative researchers' worldviews tend toward a single representation of truth, qualitative researchers usually embrace multiple truths (cf. Kvale, 1995; Winter, 2000).

Thus, although social science methodologists have seen validity as a construct applied to inferences or conclusions, we offer an alternative conceptualization that encompasses the full inquiry process aligned with the tiers of intelligence and culminates in use. In the absence of absolute judgments of validity, we dismiss validity and instead propose integrity, defined as demonstrating coherence and ethical practice, and use as the determining criteria for scientific inquiry that is credible and ethical throughout, from question framing through dissemination of results to production of usable knowledge. From our perspective as researchers who primarily use qualitative methods, inquiry conducted with integrity will yield credible data, analyses, and interpretations that produce actionable findings. Such research is used. We suggest that contextualized within a specific set of inquiry and action, integrity can serve qualitative and quantitative researchers alike as the conceptual undergirding for institutional research designed to promote organizational intelligence.

Framed in this way, truth-value becomes a judgment of credibility and utility in a given context (Rallis, 2015; Rallis, Rossman, & Gajda, 2007). Whether and how people use the research at any stage depends on how well these questions, methods, data, and results fit their understanding of what is true. The knowledge that informs most of our actions and beliefs is ordinary knowledge: knowledge based not on formal research but on "common sense, casual empiricism, or thoughtful speculation and analysis… whether it is true or false, knowledge is knowledge to anyone who takes it as a basis for some commitment or action" (Lindblom & Cohen, 1979, p. 12). The overriding question asked in inquiry processes should not be: "Is it valid?" but rather "Is this a useful way of understanding, and potentially acting upon, a given problem?" The users hold the key—they determine truth or value.

How can a researcher ensure integrity and use? Although there is no single way of doing so, we suggest that by following principles for rigorous, scientific education research, both qualitative and quantitative researchers can produce work with integrity and utility. According to National Research Council's Scientific Principles for Education Research (NRC Principles) (Shavelson & Towne, 2002), scientific research studies do the following:

- Pose significant questions that can be investigated empirically
- Link research to relevant theory
- Use methods that permit direct investigation of the questions
- Provide a coherent and explicit chain of reasoning
- Replicate and generalize across studies
- Disclose research to encourage professional scrutiny and critique.

These scientific principles are foundational to the discovery of credible, usable evidence that can contribute to organizational intelligence. To illustrate our conceptualization of integrity as essential to truth-value and use, we offer a case example from our research practice that demonstrates how rigorous, systematic, and ethically conducted qualitative studies can meet the scientific principles and ultimately be used.

Our Case and Context

We were contracted to study the status of collaboration between agencies working together to educate students living and receiving their education in state-run institutional settings. We refer to the research project as Collaboration for Education in Institutionalized Settings (CEIS). Workers from various agencies (education, clinical professionals, and residential staff) needed to collaborate at the site level to create a positive educational environment for students with serious mental health challenges. This educational program operated in eight sites across the state and involved a state agency, several state contractors, and multiple education providers, including a higher education institution. At the state level, a formal commitment to collaboration in practice existed. The leadership of differing organizations met regularly to discuss collaborative efforts. When we were hired, this group asked us to create a metric through which they could measure and assess site-level collaboration.

Early in our research, we recognized that collaboration was not yet a measurable construct at the site level of this program. No mutually agreed upon definition for collaboration nor standardized practices existed within or between sites. Some workers at certain sites collaborated as a result of the natural relationship and respect that had evolved between professionals with differing roles. Other sites were characterized by almost adversarial relationships between various staff members. Our research quickly shifted from "how can we measure collaboration in these sites" to "where is collaboration occurring and how can we learn from it to inform others?"

The analysis that follows is organized according to NRC principles for scientific inquiry, correlated with Terenzini's tiers of organizational intelligence, asking: How does this principle support use? What organizational intelligence is required? We then apply these ideas to the CEIS study, asking: How did our choices align with the principle? What organizational intelligence did we use? We demonstrate how our choices within methods, theories, and presentation result in research that has integrity and thus contributes to organizational intelligence, ideally leading to credible, actionable evidence and positive organizational change.

Those who believe a research study is conducted according to principles of scientific inquiry are more likely to use the findings than those who doubt the rigor and probity of the inquiry process used. The NRC Guiding Principles can help researchers shape their work with integrity. "These principles are not a set of rigid standards for conducting and evaluating individual studies, but rather are a set of norms enforced by the community of researchers that shape scientific understanding" (Shavelson & Towne, 2002, p. 2). We suggest that these norms are accepted and enforced by relevant communities of scholars and practice because they support the ethical generation of credible and actionable knowledge.

NRC Principle 1.   According to NRC Principle 1, scientific research poses *significant questions that can be investigated empirically*. Significant questions promise use because they address the pressing problems of institutions, how the institutions function, and how decisions are made. They articulate and express organizational interests and priorities—these questions will be used because they need to be answered. Because the purposes are important, the questions will engage researchers and institutional players throughout the inquiry, resulting in use. Such significant questions fall into Terenzini's Tier 2 Issues Intelligence, which comprises "knowledge of the major issues or decision areas that face institutions and the people who manage them" (p. 4). Researchers need to be politically savvy about the issues: Who defines what is considered important? What norms apply? Whose interests are dominant? To what ends? Tier 2 involves successfully working with and understanding other people to accomplish the research goal.

Significant questions must also be answerable. To generate questions that can be investigated empirically, researchers need Terenzini's Tier 1 technical/analytical intelligence, which covers the methodological skills necessary to frame investigable questions. The skilled researcher builds questions that respond to a study's purpose; they specify what is to be measured or observed or discussed or explained or predicted.

Tier 3 contextual intelligence also contributes to formulating significant questions that can be empirically investigated. These questions understand the historical, philosophical, and political evolution of the institution. They recognize and honor ethical practice and the relational aspect of institutional research: How do the questions respect the people and their perspectives as well as the functioning of the institution? What benefits and harms might be embedded in the research questions? Are they fair? The questions must be ones people want to explore and are willing to answer. In summary, significant questions are feasible because they address required resources: time, effort and energy, skills and attitudes, support, commitment and cooperation, moral considerations, and ethical choices. In short, they have integrity and are doable (see Rossman & Rallis, 2017).

Initially, the CEIS Leadership Team asked us to assess the level of collaboration between the educational contractor and the institutional agency to provide a metric for self-evaluation. In essence, their questions were: How much collaboration among staff was occurring on site? How can the state-level Leadership Team and the site leadership measure their collaboration? The data collected quickly revealed that these were not the right questions. Developing the proposed metric was premature; we saw no clear-cut, consistent, systematic collaboration happening. Our Tier 2 issues intelligence, that is, our understanding of how organizations function and decisions are made, told us that the priority for the institutions was not measurement of collaboration but rather building a shared and practical definition of collaboration. Also, our Tier 1 technical/analytic intelligence indicated that the initial questions were not feasible—until we knew what we were looking for, how could we measure it? The immediate need of the sites was to explicate what this term *collaboration* meant to the Leadership Team and agencies, and our research questions needed to reflect this. So, we drew on our Tier 3 contextual intelligence to learn what was the culture of collaboration in this particular institution—in each site and the whole—and who were the key players (Terenzini, 1993). We used these intelligences to guide our conversations with the Leadership Team and learned much about the history that separated the staff on site, about the current political atmosphere that placed legal demand for collaboration on staff, and about the evolving philosophical perspectives toward student education and care. The result was a revised set of questions that more directly aligned with Principle 1:

1. In what ways, when, and where do personnel from both agencies already work together?
2. How do personnel perceive collaboration in their work?
3. What needs for working together do personnel in both agencies identify?
4. What capacity building do personnel need to actuate joint visions and goals?

NRC Principle 2.   The second principle of scientific inquiry *links research to relevant theory*. All research is grounded in some conceptual or theoretical framework because the very process of framing questions represents some worldview. "Theory is implicit in any human action" (Schratz & Walker, 1995, p. 105). Additionally, grounding research in relevant theories serves multiple broader purposes related to the integrity and truth-value of the study, and thus use. First, connecting research to existing theory allows researchers to use what is already known about the issues embedded in the significant questions identified in the work. The more acquainted researchers become with existing research, the more easily they can identify gaps and hone their questions and methods. It takes technical/analytical skill—Tier 1 intelligence—to identify and use appropriate theory. As researchers identify and shape theory in the context of their processes, they move through Tiers 2 (issues) and 3 (context) of organizational intelligence.

Theories—both theory and Theory—inform researchers' conceptual frameworks, the "working understanding of the topic, setting, and situation you are interested in" (Rossman & Rallis, 2017, p. 106). We differentiate between Theories, "propositions that are grounded in extensive research and accepted as explanations for particular phenomenon" (pp. 107–8), and lower-case theories that refer to personal understandings or explanations that guide practices—espoused theories and theories-in-use (see Argyris & Schon, 1978). Researchers' conceptual frameworks, when grounded in a strong theoretical base, articulate researchers' perspectives and convey "how and why [their] ideas matter relative to some larger body of ideas embodied in the research, writings, and experiences of others" (Schram, 2006, p. 58.)

Thus, linking research to theory requires researchers to use all three tiers of organizational intelligence. Researchers may ask themselves: Which theories inform what we see about the institution's issues or problems? Is it fair to draw parallels between existing theory and the issues we are seeking to understand in our context? How can our discoveries contribute to other institutional learning and policy discussions? Exploring answers to these questions asks researchers to be familiar with the issues, to know where to look for and locate relevant theory, and then to understand the context sufficiently to apply theory meaningfully to their setting. Equally important, institutional researchers have an obligation to establish the significance for their work to larger audiences than their particular institution. A strong theoretical base facilitates all three responsibilities.

Our CEIS case was informed by multiple layers of theory, including formal, recognized theories about organizational learning and change (Tier 3), and local, informal theories-in-use generated by participants (Tier 2). In our role as program evaluators, we drew on our practice as well as our knowledge of organizational change theory. Various Theories and theories informed our research process, from question formulation to data collection to presentation.

The program theory-of-action was articulated in conversations with the Leadership Team: Education is critical to the success of institutionalized students. For education in institutionalized settings to be effective, staff in all three roles (treatment, education, and residential) must see education as part of treatment and treatment as integral to education; thus, all staff must collaborate to serve the students. This theory guided the framing of research questions, data collection, and analysis. Using the theory allowed us to make sense of and critique the observed lack of collaborative activities and the absence of any definition of collaboration in the settings. Our use of theory also shaped our communication of what we discovered and our recommendations for next steps.

Although research on collaboration in institutional settings was not extensive, we found studies that offered models of potential strategies that might work in the CEIS institutions. None of the models were exactly what would be implemented in each setting; seeing models, however, allowed the Leadership Team, local leadership, and staff to recognize the presence of collaborative interactions in other settings similar to their own. Models served to enhance discussions of what was needed and what was possible for effective collaboration to occur.

We also utilized a variety of organizational theories (see Bolman & Deal, 2008) to name phenomena, practices, or decisions that staff would recognize as occurring at their sites. This reference to theories proved to be especially helpful in making our research findings relevant and useful. An illustrative example is our interpretation of one setting's move to have physical activity instead of math lessons after lunch as an instance of double-loop learning (Argyris & Schon, 1978). Students' behavior had become increasingly difficult in math class after lunch. The treatment and education staff tried various interventions, including reward and punishment strategies. None worked. Finally, a collaborative discussion suggested that these adolescents might need to do something active rather than be forced to sit in a classroom attempting to learn math. The decision to move to outdoor physical activities met with success. When we labeled the decision as double-loop learning, responses ranged from: "So that's why it worked!" to "We need to do that more."

NRC Principle 3.   The third element of scientific inquiry requires that the methods chosen permit direct investigation of the significant questions from Principle 1. Choosing an appropriate method clearly aligns with Tier 1 of Terenzini's levels of organizational intelligence, which emphasizes researchers' technical and analytic skill. Systematic scientific inquiry begins with the design and execution of rigorous data collection activities to answer research questions. Terenzini's first domain focuses on the skills institutional researchers need to design a study that can produce usable knowledge and to carry out the design—to actually do the study. Skilled researchers ground their designs in what they want to discover—in the questions. Significantly, well-written questions identify the locus of interest and point the way to a potentially useful method.

So, the key question for this principle is: Do the methods selected lead to data that will answer the question? However, issues of politics, ethics, and probity also inform design and method selection and thus raise additional questions: Are the methods driven by the questions, or by the researcher's skill set? Whose interests are served? Whose voices will be captured? Are the methods potentially intrusive, even harmful? Do they demonstrate respect for the participants? Is the method fair to participants and to those excluded? How do we effectively communicate method selection when sometimes pressure exists to select a particular method for political or symbolic reasons? In summary, is this research designed with respect, justice, and beneficence (Hemmings, 2006) regarding participants as well as potential end users? Researchers require Tier 2 issues intelligence to address these ethical and political concerns.

The method and design shape the relationships and interactions between the researcher and the participants that, in turn, affect analyses and interpretations—all aspects of whatever method is chosen. Here, Tier 2 intelligence involves knowledge of how to work successfully with other people to accomplish the research goal (Terenzini, 1993, p. 5). The moral principles underlying a design, as much as a predetermined set of data collection procedures and analytic strategies, are critical because data collection, analyses, interpretations, and findings play out in the relationships that researchers build with their participants. Rossman and Rallis (2003, 2017) note that researchers and participants are involved in continual and changing interaction. The researcher needs to ask: What might be possible consequences of my relationship with participants? Of my interpretations? What rights of participants might I violate? What potential harms might result? Are the participants likely to benefit in any way—and are they likely to agree on the benefit? To be trustworthy, the relationship must be ethical, consciously guided by explicit moral principles. Ultimately, to produce knowledge that can be used for improvement, the reflexive process invites researchers to identify their ethical perspective, ask of themselves: What are my values? What rules or standards apply? What moral principles guide my decisions? Equally critical is that the researchers question their actions: Do I act according to my principles?

Given these human effects on the research, the method, in addition to being directly investigable, must build in opportunities for reflection and revision. An appropriate method allows researchers to understand the question and data within the study's frame and also to hold themselves "open to the situation's back talk" (Schön, 1983, p. 164). They draw on their familiarity with the specific organization and are at the same time open to re-definition and insights of the particular context. As researchers engage in a reflective and reflexive process, they use Tier 3 contextual intelligence.

Our revised research questions for the CEIS project were answerable with qualitative methods. We used an ethnographic approach, guided by Erickson's (1986) four fieldwork questions. We visited eight sites over the course of the project, where we interviewed key actors and observed interactions to understand what was happening in each setting. Our theoretical framework helped us make sense of what we heard and saw.

Technically, we could have designed a study that purported to measure some artificial construct of collaboration, given that measurement was what the original study called for. We even had contracted a psychometrician to work with us, so the technical skill was within our capacity. However, the reality of the program—the context (Tier 3)—and the important issues of the site (Tier 2) called for different questions that led to a qualitative design. Importantly, the end result of that pathway we did not take—a rubric based on some artificial construct—would not have been useful in practice and would thus have lacked integrity. As researchers, we felt that taking the artificial pathway would not have been an ethical choice. Because our research team was able to access the full range of organizational intelligence within the project, we were able to select questions and methods that led to a useful process and results. The project as a whole had integrity throughout the inquiry cycle and reporting.

NRC Principle 4. According to the fourth principle, credible researchers must *provide a coherent and explicit chain of reasoning* regarding all their decisions from conceptualization through analyses and interpretations to findings. Making the reasoning transparent increases integrity and allows other researchers to examine and critique the choices made. Like the third principle, this characteristic of credible research draws on the multiple levels of organizational intelligences. First, the act of reasoning and providing transparent explanation for that reasoning requires Tier 1 technical and analytic skill. However, neither researchers nor participants examine questions and data or build meaning in a vacuum, so this principle draws on skills in the other two tiers of institutional intelligence. A researcher's chain of reasoning is shaped by understanding existing theory, institutional issues, and broader context.

Whether individually constructed or co-constructed with participants, providing consumers and potential users of the research with coherent reasoning clarifies connections between questions, data, analyses, inferences, and conclusions. A transparent chain of reasoning serves as foundation for the integrity of any inquiry process and product. Researchers can demonstrate more than coherence; making reasoning explicit also reveals moral principles on which decisions are grounded. Ethically reflexive questions researchers might ask in support of the integrity of their work include: Is the design fair to all participants? How has the data collection respected the institution and participants? Whose voices are recognized and included— or missing? Can others see what I see? Is the evidence visible for the patterns and inferences identified? What alternative interpretations of these data are possible? What influenced the selected interpretation and conclusions? Are conclusions based on data—or a byproduct of power structures or preconceived expectations? What potential benefits or harms might result from the interpretations and conclusions?

Our CEIS research was conceptualized with the theoretical perspectives we identified in our discussion of NRC Principle 2 and the project theory-of-action—and thus informed our design, data collection, analysis, and interpretation. We articulated the theory-of-action with the Leadership Team and made explicit our reasoning behind each step of the proposed research. The ongoing discussion of what we proposed and what we were doing became an iterative cycle that first exposed the lack of coherence in the purpose and design, then supported morally sound modifications, and ultimately produced results grounded in integrity.

Our reasoning related to discoveries about one obstruction to collaboration at the sites serves to illustrate. We witnessed deep separation between job roles within the institutions; therapeutic staff, residential staff, and education staff had split into three (sometimes competing or conflicting) camps. Describing this observation to the Leadership Team revealed that the three camps were an artifact of state policies that had shifted institutional governance from under management by a unified agency to management by an agency plus multiple contractors working under the purview of that agency. Each role answered to a different management system with differing rules and expectations for the work. The effect of the divisions within the agency made collaboration difficult if not impossible. To describe and explain our reasoning to the leadership and workers, we used the metaphor of camps drawing on political and symbolic influences they recognized; the metaphor offered them a visual that opened discussion of actionable and ethical alternatives.

Throughout all stages of the research, we described, explained, and often illustrated our decisions and were open to other possibilities. When we reached conclusions, we presented our analyses and interpretations in the form of PowerPoints that explained our chain of reasoning. Because the chain of reasoning was made explicit, and because it grew in coherence over the inquiry process, the findings produced were credible, actionable, and useful.

NRC Principle 5.   NRC Principle 5 calls for research to be *replicable and generalizable across studies*. Although we agree with Principle 4 that researchers have the responsibility to be transparent and coherent enough in design, execution, and conclusions that others can see (and critique) what was done, we suggest that the terms *replicate* and *generalize* are irrelevant for research conducted in the social sciences. Social science researchers, who deal with human beings, cannot exactly replicate or broadly generalize what was done with a person or group of persons at one time in one place with another (or even the same) at a different time or place. Both Tiers 2 and 3 of organizational intelligence stress the importance of issues and context awareness—and issues and contexts change over time with different people. Even with the same people in the same institution, their time and experience in the place will differ, so the context and other variables differ. Similarly, strict, probabilistic generalizing cannot be extended to any population beyond that from which the given sample was drawn. As a result, generalizability is typically not a word in a qualitative researcher's vocabulary, but what is learned in one study can be useful for other settings.

Thus, we prefer to use terms such as *transferability* or *applicability* or useability to describe the criteria that support production of credible and actionable results. Researchers draw on their Tier 1 technical/analytic intelligence to provide thick descriptions (see Geertz, 1994) with as much detail about the actions and interactions as feasible. Thick descriptions make visible patterns and allow for interpretations of what is happening. A clear and coherent chain of reasoning and thick description also make it possible for another researcher to conduct (not replicate) a similar study. "Potential users can then determine for themselves if [research] results will be of use in a new but similar setting. They compare and contrast the specifics of [the] study with their own setting and consider if the two are sufficiently similar for your findings to be insightful" (Rossman & Rallis, 2017, p. 55).

Both CEIS leadership and staff applied and used the information we provided. Replication would have been inappropriate and impossible, given the contextual variances between institutional settings. When presenting or writing our findings from one research setting, we used our Tier 1 and 2 intelligences to describe what we saw and heard with such detail that the participants readily recognized the realities of the settings—and saw how they could use what we learned in one place to improve practice in another. We described a number of promising site-generated tools and practices for facilitating cross-agency communication that we witnessed at various settings. For example, details about the "Bindex," a centralized binder of standard reporting that is reviewed by employees at one site at the beginning of a shift and annotated at the end of the shift, proved a model for other sites. Similarly, one site used their cross-function morning meeting to bring everyone up to speed on events and areas of concern during the night; this meeting was adopted by other sites. In short, our research offered thick descriptions to facilitate analogous reasoning by the program personnel.

NRC Principle 6.   The sixth principle for scientific inquiry asks researchers to *disclose research to encourage professional scrutiny and critique.* For many qualitative research practitioners, the disclosure of research to professional scrutiny and critique is a natural step. Competent, ethical researchers frequently seek input and reflection from participants and end users while the study is in progress; they are open to critique. They share with those who participate in the research and then extend the knowledge gained through the inquiry to the greater professional community. These steps provide opportunity for the institution to examine and critique research findings and create practical change from those findings. This principle aligns most closely with Tier 3 of Terenzini's organizational intelligence, which calls for contextual, system-oriented thinking to become part of knowledge production. Terenzini calls Tier 3 intelligence the "crowning form" (p. 6). The institutional researcher learning from inquiry does not suffice. To make inquiry worthwhile, others must have the opportunity to learn from the findings and take action.

This principle calls for the learning to extend beyond the institution and inform the larger scientific community. Organizational learnings optimally contribute to understanding beyond the confines of the institution. Researchers may ask themselves: How can these learnings inform what others are facing? How do these learnings inform or add to the theory base about the issue of practice addressed through this research? How can this work be useful beyond the context of the institution?

Professional scrutiny and critique was inherent to the design of both stages of the CEIS case. We attended the monthly Leadership Team meetings to update them on our progress and hear their feedback, which we would then incorporate into our efforts when appropriate. Our transparency meant that the research was used formatively by them and that their input continually shaped the study—thus strengthening the credibility of the research. From the onset, we agreed to deliver in-person presentations of our findings to key participants and stakeholders. In addition, we provided a readable and actionable executive summary of the study. These forms of findings contributed to positive, observable changes during our time working with these institutions and beyond.

We presented our findings from the initial study to institutional leaders. These findings revealed that no consistent operational definition of collaboration existed in the various sites. At the conclusion of the presentation, the agency director said, "Thank goodness somebody finally said it" (meeting notes, June 2010). Thus, they asked us to present our findings to the research participants (the staff from the various agencies at the site—a group of some 50 people), who responded positively and used the findings to talk about and change their practices in their institutions. Beyond their current practices, they used our research findings to inform the development of a new building that brought three of the eight separate institutions together. They used research findings as a form of Tier 3 intelligence.

As we identify above, Principle 6 calls for disclosure beyond the institution. We have done that through conference presentations, academic papers, and other research activities. Ultimately, the research that was initially conceptualized as creating a management tool for measurement of site-level collaboration became something much more powerful with reach beyond these institutions, because we engaged in scientifically sound, ethical inquiry—inquiry with integrity.

Conclusion

We began by exploring the idea that the use of research informed the validity of the inferences from that research; we quickly realized that previous conceptualizations of validity were too narrow to describe what leads to credible, actionable evidence—that is, use. Ultimately, we moved away from validity as a critical criterion to embrace integrity—wholeness or coherence and ethical grounding. As we applied the NRC Scientific Principles, we found that the word *validity* is only mentioned in one Principle in the Executive Summary—Principle 4, which calls for a coherent and explicit chain of reasoning for any research study—thus supporting our argument that research integrity demands more than validity.

Integrity—the quality of being honest, having strong moral principles, and a cohesive foundation—is a more apt and useful description for this way of considering the credibility of work, encompassing the full inquiry cycle of design, implementation, and use. Integrity in a researcher requires more than technical/analytical skill, or Tier 1 organizational intelligence. Integrity requires that the processes, from the framing of questions, to the relationships with participants, to the inferences and conclusions, have coherence, addressing important issues of the institution in contextually appropriate ways.

We conclude our chapter with a return to our original emphasis on use. Research integrity through all three tiers of organizational intelligence provides a framework, and researchers can use the six principles as a guide for decision-making during the full inquiry process. Doing so requires technical skill as well as awareness of what is important to the site and to the larger context. Because the reasoning will be made explicit, its moral soundness and coherence can be judged. When audiences for the research deem the research to have integrity, they are more likely to accept it as credible and to use it. The resulting use of knowledge generated from scientifically principled inquiry is further testimony to the integrity of that work: the results have truth-value, the organization can make sense of that truth-value, and ultimately act on that value.

References

Argyris, C., & Schon, D. A. (1978). *Organizational learning: A theory-of-action perspective*. Reading, MA: Addison-Wesley.

Bolman, L. G., & Deal, T. E. (2008). *Reframing organizations: Artistry, choice, and leadership* (4th ed.). San Francisco, CA: Jossey-Bass.

Cho, J., & Trent, A. (2006). Validity in qualitative research revisited. *Qualitative Research, 6*(3), 319–340.

Erickson, F. (1986). Qualitative methods in research on teaching. In M. C. Whittrock (Ed.), *Handbook of research on teaching* (3rd ed., pp. 119–161). New York, NY: MacMillian.

Foucault, M., & Blasius, M. (1993). About the beginning of the hermeneutics of the self: Two lectures at Dartmouth. *Political Theory, 21*(2), 198–227.

Geertz, C. (1994). Thick description: Toward an interpretive theory of culture. *Readings in the Philosophy of Social Science*, 213–231.

Hemmings, A. (2006). Great ethical divides: Bridging the gap between institutional review boards and researchers. *Educational Researcher, 35*(4), 12–18.

Heshusius, L. (1994). Free ourselves from objectivity: Managing subjectivity or toward a participatory mode of consciousness? *Educational Researcher, 23*(3), 15–22.

Kvale, S. (1995). The social construction of validity. *Qualitative Inquiry, 1*(1), 19–40.

Lindblom, C., & Cohen, D. K. (1979). *Usable knowledge: Social science and social problem solving*. New Haven, CT: Yale University Press.

Maxwell, J. A. (1992). Understanding validity in qualitative research. *Harvard Educational Review, 62*(3), 279–300.

Onwuegbuzie, A. J., & Leech, N. L. (2007). Validity and qualitative research: An oxymoron?. *Quality & Quantity, 41*(2), 233–249.

Peshkin, A. (1988). In search of subjectivity—One's own. *Educational Researcher, 17*(7), 17–21.

Rallis, S. F. (2015). When and how qualitative methods provide credible and actionable evidence: Reasoning with rigor, probity, and transparency. In S. Donaldson, C. Christie, & M. Mark (Eds.), *Credible and actionable evidence: Foundations of rigorous and influential evaluations*. Thousand Oaks, CA: Sage.

Rallis, S. F., Rossman, G. B., & Gajda, R. (2007). Trustworthiness in evaluation practice: An emphasis on the relational. *Evaluation and Program Planning, 30*(4), 404–409.

Ratcliffe, J. W. (1983). Notions of validity in qualitative research methodology. *Knowledge Creation, Diffusion, Utilization, 5*(2), 147–167.

Ratner, C. (2002). Subjectivity and objectivity in qualitative methodology. *Forum Qualitative Sozialforschung/Forum: Qualitative Social Research, 3*(3).

Rossman, G. B., & Rallis, S. F. (2003). *Learning in the field: An introduction to qualitative research* (2nd ed.). Thousand Oaks, CA: Sage.

Rossman, G. B., & Rallis, S. F. (2017). *An introduction to qualitative research: Learning in the field* (4th ed.). Thousand Oaks, CA: Sage.

Schon, D. (1983). *The reflective practitioner: How professionals think in action*. New York, NY: Basic Books.

Schram, T. H. (2006). *Conceptualizing and proposing qualitative research* (2nd ed.). Upper Saddle River, NJ: Pearson Merrill.

Schratz, M., & Walker, R. (1995). *Research as social change: New opportunities for qualitative research*. London, England: Routledge.

Shadish, W., Cook, T., & Campbell, D. (2002). *Experimental and quasi-experimental designs for generalized causal inference*. Boston, MA: Houghton Mifflin.

Shavelson, R., & Towne, L. (Eds.). (2002). *Scientific research in education*. Washington, DC: Committee on Scientific Principles for Education Research, National Research Council.

Terenzini, P. T. (1993). On the nature of institutional research and the knowledge and skills it requires. *Research in Higher Education, 34*(1), 1–10.

Winter, G. (2000). A comparative discussion of the notion of "validity" in qualitative and quantitative research. *The Qualitative Report, 4*(3), 1–14.

SHARON F. RALLIS is the Dwight W. Allen distinguished professor in education policy and reform at the University of Massachusetts Amherst.

RACHAEL B. LAWRENCE is a postdoctoral fellow in the center for education policy at the University of Massachusetts Amherst.

3

This chapter describes a process for assessing programmatic initiatives with broad-ranging goals with the use of a mixed-methods design. Using an example of a day-long teaching development conference, this chapter provides practitioners step-by-step guidance on how to implement this assessment process.

Using Mixed Methods to Assess Initiatives With Broad-Based Goals

Karen Kurotsuchi Inkelas

Higher education has been under scrutiny for several decades (Shavelson, 2010; Trow, 1998). Increasingly, external constituencies demand institutional accountability from universities and colleges to provide evidence that students are learning, that they are fiscally responsible, and that all activities and practices are mission driven (Borden & Pike, 2008; Ewell, 2008; Schmidtlein & Berdahl, 2005). To respond to these demands, institutions have turned to increasingly ambitious initiatives and the subsequent assessment of those initiatives to inform their decisions and to demonstrate effectiveness externally and internally (Shavelson, 2010). However, measuring effectiveness can be challenging when an initiative's goals are broad and diffuse.

On these occasions, institutional researchers (or those tasked to assess broad and diffuse initiatives) may need to think strategically through the lens of Terenzini's (1993) second form of organizational intelligence: issues intelligence. Institutional leaders, and those who support them, need to convey that they are both actively addressing the most pressing concerns facing higher education and showing results in improving the current condition. Thus, institutional researchers tasked in the evaluation of a broad-based initiative need to tap their issues intelligence in developing a research design that will yield results that can be used to show effectiveness, but also be rigorous and useful for programming purposes. This chapter will describe an innovative, mixed-methods assessment design that can be used both (a) to provide evidence of an initiative's effectiveness in changing behaviors (summative assessment), and (b) to inform decision-making for future programming needs (formative assessment).

NEW DIRECTIONS FOR INSTITUTIONAL RESEARCH, no. 174 © 2017 Wiley Periodicals, Inc.
Published online in Wiley Online Library (wileyonlinelibrary.com) • DOI: 10.1002/ir.20219

The Challenge With Assessing Broad-Based Initiatives

Although it is optimal to create programs or initiatives with a clear and operationalized set of goals and objectives so that the assessment of the program is based upon the fulfillment of those goals and objectives, institutions are often apt to create ambitious programming with vague or broad and diffuse purposes, making its assessment challenging. There are plenty of examples of initiatives with wide-ranging goals: for example, training to improve institutional leadership, retreats to reform a curriculum, and workshops to facilitate more effective college teaching. Although it is laudable for institutions to desire to improve upon their leadership, refresh and update their curricula, and help instructors be more effective teachers, the goals for such processes are multifaceted and complex.

Consider programs designed to help college instructors be more effective teachers. Although autonomy with teaching college courses rests with the faculty members, universities began offering instructional development programs as early as the 1960s to help professors learn more about pedagogical practices that can enhance one's teaching effectiveness. Programs often blossomed into centers, especially at large universities, and by 1994, approximately one third of colleges and universities had a formal center for teaching improvement, including 61% of research universities. These centers provide a range of programs, resources, and services, including individual teaching consultations, grants and incentives to motivate faculty to change their teaching practices, print and electronic resources on the scholarship of teaching and learning, and a variety of programs—from workshops to guest speakers to learning communities ("Centers for Teaching Improvement," n.d.; Gaff & Simpson, 1994; Wright, 2000).

Sometimes, when external constituencies question the quality or value of college instruction, institutional leaders may react by mandating that teaching centers offer ambitious events that attract the participation of a large number of faculty, but these types of events—in order to meet the interests of a wide swath of faculty—tend to become very broad based. Indeed, what should such a broad-based initiative make as its focal point? Should it focus on helping instructors develop meaningful, developmentally appropriate, and feasible course goals and objectives? Or, more specifically, should the focus be on helping instructors integrate course goals and objectives into the actual organization and functioning of the course? Or, should the focus of the workshop be on effectively executing the course instruction? Should instructors be learning how to create effective learning environments in their classroom, through concepts like learner-centered pedagogy, active learning exercises, or collaborative-based learning? Or, should the focus be on assisting instructors to be active assessors of their own classes, garnering constructive feedback from their students and making live-time changes to the class? Oftentimes, teaching development workshops do not have a singular focus, or even a combination of foci of the above elements. Instead, institutions may choose to develop single-occasion programming on "improving college teaching" without developing goals and objectives that further define and refine which aspects of teaching they wish to address.

The problematic nature of the continued creation of these broad-based programs with little regard to concrete goals and objectives notwithstanding, another challenge with these types of initiatives is how to assess them. Often, the foci of these initiatives can be high stakes (such as leadership, diversity, and teaching, to name a few), and thus there is a demand to assess their effectiveness. Yet, the vexing question is: Without knowing what the specific goals and objectives of the initiatives are, what exactly are we assessing the effectiveness of? In the past, program evaluators may have sidestepped this dilemma by relying upon other types of assessment measures. For example, some may have conflated effectiveness with relevance, and argued that if a program was well attended, enough stakeholders must have thought the topic to be important enough to warrant its continued need for programming. Others might have evaluated participants' satisfaction with the programming, or their self-perceptions about what they learned (Schuh & Associates, 2008). Higher education today, however, faces increased demands for accountability and limited funds for its operation, and thus requires more than merely taking attendance or asking about levels of satisfaction: What is now expected is proof that the initiative actually changed some aspect of institutional practice for the better—that there is a return on investment (Banta & Palomba, 2014). So the vexing question remains: What exactly are we assessing the effectiveness of?

Key Concepts in Higher Education Program Assessment

Before describing one innovative method through which the answer to the above question can be addressed, it is important to define the difference between formative and summative assessment and to introduce a model for studying programmatic effectiveness. First, in broad terms, formative assessment provides feedback to inform immediate improvement of a program or event, whereas summative assessment informs judgments about a program's or event's adoption, continuation, expansion, or overall worth (Fitzpatrick, Sanders, & Worthen, 2011). The former is usually conducted during the development or delivery of an event or program, and the latter is conducted at its end (Mertens & Wilson, 2012).

Program or initiative assessments can take different forms, but few focus on assessing actual impact. Although their model is meant to be used specifically with training programs, Kirkpatrick and Kirkpatrick (2016) offer a standard for evaluating the overall effectiveness of a program in four levels. Level One, or Reaction, assesses the degree to which participants liked the program. Level Two, Learning, concerns the degree to which participants gained the knowledge, skills, and abilities intended through the programming. Level Three, Behavior, measures the degree to which participants applied what they learned from the program back in their workplaces. Finally, Level Four, Results, studies the degree to which intended outcomes occur in the workplace because of the programming.

An Example: A One-Day Faculty Development Conference

The example presented in this chapter describes a mixed-methods assessment of a one-day conference (hereinafter referred to as the "Conference") on teaching practices held at a large, public, R1 university in the eastern United States. The goals of the Conference were broad and diffuse, but the assessment charge was to assist the initiative developers in identifying the strengths and areas of improvement of the Conference for future years' implementation (formative), and to demonstrate the Conference's overall impact on instructional efforts at the institution (summative). Although the program described in this chapter was a one-day conference focusing on teaching practices, the assessment design described in this chapter can be used in a variety of contexts for a diversity of purposes. Those interested in learning how to assess an initiative with broad-based goals, as well as use the assessment results to inform and improve future practice, can consider adopting a similar research design for their efforts.

The goal of the Conference was to highlight teaching innovations to faculty teaching at the institution, particularly instructional approaches that engage students as partners in teaching and learning. The Conference took place in May 2015. Briefly, it featured two key notes, a plenary panel, and 10 concurrent sessions, all led by different faculty. The two key notes and the plenary panel were joint sessions attended by all the Conference participants, but the 10 concurrent sessions were all held during one of two time slots. Thus, Conference participants did not all attend the same concurrent sessions. The goals of each session varied considerably, ranging from syllabus construction to service learning activities to teaching assistant training to contemplative pedagogical practices. Like many gatherings for which there are multiple sessions about an expansive topic such as teaching effectiveness, although there was an overarching theme for the Conference, the topics and goals/objectives for the sessions that comprised it varied widely.

To assess the impact of the Conference successfully without a unified set of goals and objectives, the assessment for this event included a two-phase data collection and analysis design, aimed at understanding the impact that attendance at the Conference had on subsequent classroom teaching practices at the institution. Data collection for the first assessment occurred during the Conference. The second, follow-up assessment occurred several months after the Conference. The next two sections describe the methods utilized for each phase of the assessment.

Initial Assessment.   The goal of the initial assessment was to understand better what the participants learned at the Conference, regardless of which sessions they attended. Instead of predetermining which items to include on the assessment form, participants were asked simply to list, in their own words, up to three ideas or concepts they learned at the Conference that they intended to incorporate into their own teaching. The latter half of the statement was important to include, because the assessment was charged to measure the impact of the Conference on subsequent teaching at the university. Accordingly, as the Kirkpatrick and Kirkpatrick (2016) four-level model describes, it is not only critical to assess what individuals learned (Level Two), but also how they may have incorporated what they learned into their workplace (Level Three) to estimate impact. Thus, it is important to ask the Conference participants to list only those concepts that they planned to incorporate into their teaching so that these concepts can be queried again later. Data for the initial assessment were collected during the Conference via a paper-and-pencil form. The assessment form was distributed to participants during every session of the Conference.

Sample.   A total of 209 individuals attended the Conference. Of those, 119 completed the initial assessment instrument, for a 57% response rate. Although most respondents were faculty members, staff members, graduate students, and undergraduate students also attended the Conference and responded to the initial assessment. Nearly half of the respondents were affiliated with the university's College of Arts and Sciences, 35% worked in one of the other schools or colleges, and 14% were from the university's central administration or were instructors from another, nearby institution. Among the faculty attending the Conference, about half were of a non–tenure-track rank (lecturer or instructor), and there was a mix of respondents from the ranks of assistant professors, associate professors, and full professors. Most respondents were female (64%), and 35% were between the ages of 25 and 34, 27% between 35 and 44, and 21% between 45 and 54.

Data Analysis.   Responses to the initial assessment form were entered into a Microsoft Excel spreadsheet. The qualitative responses to the question regarding what respondents learned at the Conference that they intended to incorporate into their teaching represented a wide range of concepts, 364 in all. Two independent coders began the analysis by sorting respondents' responses into categories. Once the two coders had separately finished an initial category formation, a larger group of four reviewed the independent coders' work, and through consensus, created a final, combined set of categories. The group emerged with a total of seven categories, each including several subcategories. Each category was given a title (e.g., a concept related to "teaching with technology"). To ensure accuracy, the two independent coders re-sorted the original 364 responses into the seven categories and subcategories. The result of the re-sorting process uncovered the need to readjust a few categories to reflect the data better. Once the two coders were in agreement with all 364 responses belonging to the same categories in the re-sorting process, the first phase of data analysis was completed.

Follow-Up Assessment.   To study the impact that the Conference had on participants regarding their teaching practices, a follow-up data collection was administered in the early Spring 2016 semester (January–February 2016) via an online survey. The decision to conduct the follow-up assessment in January 2016 was based upon the premise that instructors teaching in the Fall 2015 and/or Spring 2016 semesters will have had at least one and perhaps two terms to implement what they learned from the Conference into their teaching. In addition to basic demographic questions, the follow-up assessment instrument consisted of seven questions. These seven questions were based on the seven categories developed from the analysis of the question from the initial assessment: "What three ideas/concepts did you learn at the Conference that you intend to incorporate into your teaching?" For each category of ideas or concepts related to teaching practices, participants indicated whether they had (a) incorporated this idea/concept into their teaching since the Conference; (b) already been using this idea/concept in their teaching prior to the Conference; (c) an abiding interest in incorporating this idea/concept into their teaching but had not yet done so. Participants also had the option to indicate whether the idea/concept was not applicable to their teaching, was not of interest to them, or if they were unfamiliar with what the idea/concept was.

Figure 3.1 provides an example of one of the survey items on the follow-up assessment. One of the seven categories created from the initial assessment was a desire to incorporate more reflective activities into one's teaching. In addition, there were three subcategories created for the reflection category: (a) incorporating student reflective writing and/or journaling; (b) using mindfulness techniques; and (c) using prompts, such as chimes or bells. The resulting survey question on the follow-up instrument is illustrated in Figure 3.1.

Sample.   An online link to the follow-up assessment was emailed to all registrants of the May 2015 Conference in January 2016. Because not all the registrants attended the Conference, the first question on the survey asked respondents if they attended. If respondents answered "no," they were exited from the online survey. A total of 60 individuals completed the follow-up assessment, for a 29% response rate. Approximately two thirds of the follow-up respondents were affiliated with the College of Arts and Sciences, with the majority being faculty members of varying ranks. Most respondents were women (60%), with one third being between the ages of 25 and 44 and one third between the ages of 45 and 54. In comparing the demographic profile of respondents from the initial assessment to the follow-up assessment, the follow-up sample is slightly overrepresented by members of the College of Arts and Science and is slightly older in age. In addition, among the faculty in both assessments, the follow-up sample is composed of a greater proportion of tenure and tenure-track professors, whereas the initial assessment had a higher proportion of non–tenure-track respondents.

Figure 3.1. Sample question from follow-up assessment instrument.

Incorporating more reflection
Please indicate whether you have incorporated the following items into your teaching.

	Incorporating this into my teaching since Conference in May 2015	Already doing this in my teaching prior to May 2015	Interested in incorporating this into my teaching, but have not yet done so	Not interested in this	Not applicable	What is this?
Incorporating student reflective writing and/or journaling	○	○	○	○	○	○
Using mindfulness techniques	○	○	○	○	○	○
Using prompts (e.g., chimes or bells)	○	○	○	○	○	○

Data Analysis.   The data from the follow-up assessment were broken out into several domains: the first set of analyses reported on new ideas or concepts being used in respondents' teaching practices that they learned about from the Conference. These results represent one form of summative evaluation, because the ideas or concepts identified from these findings are those that were acquired from the Conference. Thus, it may be inferred that these findings represent the "impact" of the Conference. It is important to note, however, that responses to the initial and follow-up assessments were not linked because of the decision to preserve the anonymity of the respondents. Thus, instructors using certain ideas or concepts in their teaching after the Conference may not be the same ones who identified those ideas or concepts on the initial assessment. Nevertheless, one benefit of this method of analysis is that it is possible to ascertain the extent to which all instructors are using certain ideas or concepts in their teaching, instead of a select few who identified them as something they learned at the Conference. The second set of analyses depicted which ideas or concepts respondents had indicated they had already incorporated into their teaching prior to the Conference. Although these findings did not necessarily illustrate what new ideas or concepts instructors learned at the Conference, they did exemplify popular teaching practices used at the institution.

The third set of analyses revealed ideas or concepts learned at the Conference that respondents were interested in using but had not yet incorporated into their teaching, and the fourth set of analyses identified ideas or concepts that respondents had no interest in using in their teaching. Finally, the fifth set of analyses reported on ideas or concepts that at least some Conference participants stated in the initial assessment that they learned about and planned to use in their teaching, but that some respondents to the follow-up assessment were not familiar with or did not recognize. This last set of findings is not surprising, given that there were 10 concurrent sessions at the Conference, meaning that not all participants attended the same sessions and learned about the same things.

The above three sets of analyses can serve as effective types of formative assessment: for example, identifying which ideas or concepts respondents had no interest in can signal which topics to avoid for future conferences or similar types of initiatives. Similarly, those ideas or concepts that significant numbers of respondents did not recognize but were institutional priorities may be an indication of areas in which stakeholders will need additional introductory training. Finally, those ideas or concepts for which respondents had interest but had not yet implemented in their work represents topic areas the university can invest in for targeted training, in other words, training that focuses less on introducing topics and more on tips for implementing them.

NEW DIRECTIONS FOR INSTITUTIONAL RESEARCH • DOI: 10.1002/ir

Summative and Formative Results From Our Example

Categories Emerging From the Initial Assessment. As previously described, respondents were provided open-ended blanks to free-write any ideas or concepts they learned at the Conference that they intended to incorporate into their teaching practices. To review, there were 364 ideas/concepts provided in the initial assessment, which were subsequently sorted into seven categories with respective subcategories. Below is the full list of categories and subcategories from the initial assessment:

1. Using new technologies

   Subcategories:

   Using ePortfolios
   Developing blogs
   Using more functions in course management system
   Using learning catalytics
   Using new technology equipment

2. Creating active and interactive learning environments

   Subcategories:

   Using games
   Using one-point reading quizzes
   Creating purposeful activities
   Allowing greater student autonomy regarding readings

3. Employing learner-centered pedagogies

   Subcategories:

   Using a flipped classroom
   Using problem-based learning
   Having students learn through conducting their own research
   Tips on improving class participation

4. Facilitating peer learning

   Subcategories:

   Having students write for one another
   Incorporating more small group work

5. Incorporating more reflection

   Subcategories:

   Incorporating student reflective writing and journaling
   Using mindfulness techniques
   Using prompts (e.g., bells or chimes)

6. Facilitating difficult topics and using greater empathy

   Subcategories:

   Using writing to explore controversial issues
   Creating safe spaces in the classroom

Allowing students to learn by trial and error without repercussions

Being more approachable during stressful times

Referring students to University resources when called for

7. Doing ongoing teaching development

Subcategories:

Conducting mid-semester student evaluations

Using "takeaways"

Attending more teaching workshops, including on line

Creating professional development opportunities for TAs/graduate students

Among the most popular subcategories of responses were (a) incorporating student reflective writing and journaling (7%), (b) providing students more autonomy over their own teaching (6%), (c) using a flipped classroom (6%), (d) using new technology equipment (5%), and (e) allowing greater student autonomy regarding readings (4%). Hence, in terms of formative evaluation, one might infer that these were the five most popular ideas or concepts learned at the Conference.

Findings From the Follow-Up Assessment.   The follow-up data collection allowed us to learn which of the above-enumerated ideas or concepts were incorporated into instructors' teaching, or the actual impact of the Conference on teaching practices at the institution. Among all the subcategories, the following concepts were the most often incorporated into participants' teaching after the Conference: (a) improving class participation (25%), (b) using more functions in the course management system (17%), (c) using purposeful classroom activities (16%), and (d) incorporating student reflective writing and journaling (12%). Interestingly, only one of the five most popular responses (incorporating student reflective writing and journaling) provided in the initial assessment turned out to be one of the most prevalently adopted teaching practices in actuality. Nonetheless, the above results show that between 12% and 25% of Conference attendees did change some aspect of their teaching practices because of something they learned at the Conference. It is also important to note that between 55% and 72% of respondents indicated that they were already using many of the ideas or concepts covered in the Conference in their teaching, such as using small group work (72%) or referring students to University resources (e.g., the Counseling Center) when called for (6%).

There were also concepts identified by respondents that they were interested in adopting, but had not yet done so, including: (a) mindfulness techniques (46%), (b) new technology/equipment (39%), (c) one-point reading quizzes (36%), and (d) "takeaways" (3%). Although the reasons for not using these practices are unknown, possible explanations might include an instructor's lack of time to think through how to integrate these activities into his or her existing classes, or a lack of confidence in adopting a new teaching practice, or a need for further assistance in learning how to use such practices in one's teaching. These reasons can be rectified by the institution by providing targeted resources to instructors, such as providing small teaching grants to buy out faculty time to work on course design or redesign, or workshops run by the university's teaching center on how to implement specific teaching pedagogies into one's courses.

Finally, there were some teaching practices that respondents were unfamiliar with, such as using blogs (29%), games (28%), ePortfolios (26%), or one-point reading quizzes (24%) in classes. Institutional offices devoted to working with instructors on their teaching, such as teaching centers or programs that focus on instructional technology, can take note of faculty members' lack of knowledge in these areas and begin to think of effective ways to introduce them to such concepts.

Using This Assessment Method to Inform and Improve Practice

Despite there being no unifying set of objectives for the Conference on teaching innovations, the assessment of the Conference was based on twin goals: (a) to understand the impact that attendance the Conference had on participants' actual teaching practices, and (b) to obtain feedback from participants on teaching practices they would like to learn more about through similar professional development activities. Summatively speaking, the follow-up assessment showed that between 12% and 25% of Conference attendees had adopted at least one idea or concept learned from the Conference into their teaching practices. Thus, the Conference did have an impact on teaching at the institution.

In terms of formative results, there were specific teaching practices that instructors found noteworthy but for whatever reason had not yet integrated them into their teaching. Moreover, there were some teaching practices that instructors stated were unfamiliar to them, but were identified as good teaching practices by either the literature or the university itself. These practices would appear to be of high priority for those units at the institution whose mission it is to improve teaching, such as the teaching center, offices that specialize in the use of technology in teaching, and even mindfulness centers when it comes to reflective practices. In addition, these very same units can now tailor the developmental needs of their clients by knowing which topics might require a more introductory treatment (in other words, those which are unfamiliar to the instructors) and which topics may require more narrowly tailored training (such as those for which instructors already have an expressed interest, but may need assistance on implementation or confidence-building). Finally, for those topics that critical masses of instructors found to be of little to no interest, teaching centers and similar units may consider placing less emphasis on those areas in their future programming.

New Directions for Institutional Research • DOI: 10.1002/ir

Benefits of Assessment Method for a Wide Range of Contexts. Assessing an initiative with broad and diffuse goals can be challenging. Yet, in today's climate of assessment in higher education, this is exactly what programs and initiatives are being asked to do. The two-phase assessment design described in this chapter features many advantages to programs facing similar assessment challenges. First, when an initiative's goals and objectives are not explicitly articulated, it is difficult to even know if participants can corroborate them. Accordingly, instead of assuming which of the many diffuse goals participants learned at an initiative, this assessment design allows participants the agency to identify themselves what they learned through an open-ended question. Asking participants to use their own words to describe what they learned from an initiative satisfies Level Two of the Kirkpatrick and Kirkpatrick (2016) model of assessing program effectiveness (Learning) and sets up the ability to assess Levels Three and Four, Behavior and Results, respectively.

The additional benefit of allowing the participants themselves to identify their areas of priority for their future work is that it allows key stakeholders the opportunity to learn which topics their participants find important. Again, Terenzini (1993) referenced this kind of knowledge as issues intelligence, or the awareness of the primary issues an institution faces. In the above example, this assessment design uncovered the teaching pedagogies of highest interest to an institution's faculty. In turn, now the institution, through offices such as centers for teaching improvement and information technology, can better assist its faculty in reaching its instructional potential by providing targeted information and resources on the identified pedagogies, instead of guessing what the faculty's needs and wishes are.

Then, institutional researchers can begin the process of assessing impact by constructing follow-up assessment questions based upon what the respondents themselves stated they learned in the initial assessment. The follow-up evaluation can be administered some time after the initiative to took place to allow for the participants to adopt the practices into their work. Investigating whether or not participants integrated what they learned from the initiative into their work allows programs to assess the relative impact of the initiative on both individuals and the workplace environment, collectively. Finally, in addition to ascertaining whether the participants incorporated some concepts into their teaching, asking questions related to lingering interest in and understanding of various concepts allows program developers at the institution to learn more about concepts they could emphasize in future programming, augmenting even further a sense of institutional issues awareness.

In addition to examining teaching practices, this process can be used for a variety of programs or initiatives with broad and diffuse goals, especially those designed to have participants apply what they learned to specific tasks, such as leadership training, curriculum planning, diversity initiatives, student learning outcomes, as well as search and hiring procedures. The data from this assessment process can yield both formative and summative findings, and by adopting a complementary approach in the two-phase assessment design, the formative and summative assessments enhanced one another (Fitzpatrick et al., 2011; Smith & Barclay, 2010).

This assessment design and process, however, is not expeditious and can be labor intensive. The follow-up phase of the design must be conducted with an enough time lapse to allow for the program participants the opportunity to integrate what they learned into their work. Thus, the findings suggesting the impact of the initiative will not be immediately known. However, one might argue that any rigorous method of assessing impact cannot be instantly measured. In addition, collapsing and organizing open-ended statements into categories is a time-intensive process, especially if there are numerous numbers of statements generated, more than one independent coder doing the initial sorting, and a team of researchers working collaboratively to find consensus with the final set of categories. Yet, to construct a rigorous set of categories, the process must be careful and deliberate, implying that speed should not be the goal of this step in the process. Despite these limitations, this assessment design proved to not only be adept and comprehensive, but also flexible and inexpensive, making it easy to implement as a method through which to examine an initiative's overall impact, no matter how broad-based its focus may be.

References

Banta, T. W., & Palomba, C. A. (2014). *Assessment essentials: Planning, implementing, and improving assessment in higher education.* San Francisco, CA: Jossey-Bass.

Borden, V. M. H., & Pike, G. R. (2008). Sharing responsibility for student learning. *New Directions for Institutional Research, 2008*(S1), 83–89.

Centers for teaching improvement in colleges and universities—Terms, history, resources and services, leadership and constituencies, assumptions and impact. (n.d.). Retrieved from http://education.stateuniversity.com/pages/1818/Centers-Teaching-Improvement-in-Colleges-Universities.html

Ewell, P. T. (2008). Assessment and accountability in America today: Background and context. *Directions for Institutional Research, 2008*(S1), 7–17.

Fitzpatrick, J. L., Sanders, J., & Worthen, B. R. (2011). *Program evaluation: Alternative approaches and practical guidelines* (4th ed.). Boston, MA: Pearson.

Gaff, J. G., & Simpson, R. D. (1994). Faculty development in the United States. *Innovative Higher Education, 18*, 167–176.

Kirkpatrick, J. D., & Kirkpatrick, W. K. (2016). *Kirkpatrick's four levels of training evaluation.* Alexandria, VA: Association for Talent Development.

Mertens, D. M., & Wilson, A. T. (2012). *Program evaluation theory and practice: A comprehensive guide.* New York, NY: The Guilford Press.

Schmidtlein, F. A., & Berdahl, R. O. (2005). Autonomy and accountability: Who controls academe? In P. G. Altbach, R. O. Berdahl, & P. J. Gumport (Eds.), *American higher education in the twenty-first century: Social, political, and economic challenges* (2nd ed., pp. 71–90). Baltimore, MA: The Johns Hopkins University Press.

Schuh, J. H. & Associates. (2008). *Assessment methods for student affairs*. San Francisco, CA: Jossey-Bass.

Shavelson, R. J. (2010). *Measuring college learning responsibly: Accountability in a new era*. Stanford, CA: Stanford University Press.

Smith, K. H., & Barclay, R. D. (2010). Documenting student learning: Valuing the process. In G. L. Kramer & R. L. Swing (Eds.), *Higher education assessments: Leadership matters* (pp. 95–117). Lanham, MD: Rowan & Littlefield.

Terenzini, P. T. (1993). On the nature of institutional research and skills it requires. *Research in Higher Education*, 34(1), 1–10.

Trow, M. (1998). On the accountability of higher education in the United States. In W. G. Bowen & H. T. Shapiro (Eds.), *Universities and their leadership* (pp. 15–61). Princeton, NJ: Princeton University Press.

Wright, D. L. (2000). Faculty development centers in research universities: A study of resources and programs. In M. Kaplan (Ed.), *To improve the academy* (Vol. 19). Bolton, MA: Anker.

KAREN KUROTSUCHI INKELAS *is an associate professor of higher education in the Curry School of Education at the University of Virginia.*

NEW DIRECTIONS FOR INSTITUTIONAL RESEARCH • DOI: 10.1002/ir

4

This chapter describes a qualitative study focused on the experiences of students with disabilities within the postsecondary learning environment. Reporting unexpected findings related to athletics, it makes the case that qualitative methods are well-suited for revealing information about minoritized student populations.

Using Qualitative Research to Document Variations in Student Experience

Rachel E. Friedensen, Byron P. McCrae, Ezekiel Kimball

Much, though not all, of institutional research uses quantitative methods. Indeed, institutional research often adheres to a basic belief offered by postpositivist science: quantification not only gives us a picture of the topic of study that is relatively close to reality, but also that this picture can inform both the creation of theory and sound practice. However, recent educational research suggests that although quantitative methods can accurately capture student experiences, they capture the experiences of some students better than others (e.g., Faircloth, Alcantar, & Stage, 2015; Vaccaro, Kimball, Ostiguy, & Wells, 2015). Unfortunately, the students who are most at risk for being missed by trend-oriented quantitative data analyses are those students who hold institutionally minoritized identities.

This chapter argues that postpositivist quantitative research seeks to routinize and normalize the vagaries of social processes (Lagemann, 2002; Porter, 1995). The focus on normalizing results to fit a bell curve means that those students with widely divergent experiences are not represented; they can only be represented by studies and data sets that intended to capture data about their experiences from the outset (cf. Luker, 2008; Vaccaro et al., 2015). Far from representing a form of standardized error, those students whose voices are not captured by broad applications of quantitative approaches require deliberate attention on the behalf of institutional researchers. Using examples drawn from a qualitative study of students with nonapparent disabilities and their experiences in the postsecondary educational environment at a public research university in the northeast, this chapter demonstrates how qualitative evidence can add depth to quantitative information about what is generally true of all students while also complicating that messaging by describing differences in experience for a

NEW DIRECTIONS FOR INSTITUTIONAL RESEARCH, no. 174 © 2017 Wiley Periodicals, Inc.
Published online in Wiley Online Library (wileyonlinelibrary.com) • DOI: 10.1002/ir.20220

specific group of students. Specifically, we look at data gathered about the athletic participation of students with disabilities to deepen both what we know about students with disabilities and student athletes. Even though this seems like an innocuous example, it exposes both the ways that higher education could more fully serve students with disabilities, as well as gaps in what we can know from institutional research—namely, student with disability participation in college athletics.

We start first with a brief discussion of the tenets of postpositivist science, focusing specifically on the ways that sampling differs between quantitative and qualitative studies. We then describe an example drawn from our study of how students with disabilities experience the postsecondary learning environment and conclude with a discussion of the ways that qualitative institutional research that documents differences in student experiences helps us move from technical to contextual intelligence.

Postpositivist Science and Sampling Methods

Postpositivism developed in reaction to critiques of positivism's overwhelming commitment to objectivity and value-free neutrality, as well as its belief in human ability to determine truth (Popper, 1935/2002). Unlike positivism, postpositivists maintain that knowledge is filtered through humans first and that the social world may never be fully understood (Popper, 1935/2002). Postpositivism rejects the idea that researchers can be entirely separate from the phenomenon being investigated (Popper, 1935/2002). Rather, postpositivist researchers understand themselves as participating in the social world that they are studying, although they do continue to believe that, with each research endeavor, they add to an ever-increasing fund of knowledge (Popper, 1935/2002).

Postpositivism also uses theory to both enhance objectivity and to accurately explain social phenomena. Kuhn (1977) suggested that theories need to be accurate, consistent, broad, simple, and fruitful in order to be useful. Ultimately, a postpositivist believes that with a fairly well-attenuated theory, one would be able to understand the predictable ways that individuals, such as students in an institution, will act. Taleb (2007) nicknamed this belief the Great Intellectual Fraud, because "the bell curve ignores large deviations, cannot handle them, yet makes us confident that we have tamed uncertainty" (p. xxiv). Indeed, Taleb (2007) argued that social scientists have been operating for some time under the assumption that they can measure uncertainty by normalizing it—and that they are wrong. That mistaken assumption means that social scientists cannot predict outliers and, thus, cannot predict the outcome of events. Similarly, Popper (1935/2002) argued the falsification tenet of postpositivism, which maintains that, although scientists can never fully prove a theory, they can prove that it is demonstrably false.

New Directions for Institutional Research • DOI: 10.1002/ir

Porter (1995) critiqued postpositivist, as well as positivist, science not because it is wrong, but because its practitioners, supporters, and critics alike do not satisfactorily acknowledge the ways that quantification is a strategy of communication that is meant to grapple with distance and create a discursive, disciplinary community. Numbers—things that have been measured and quantified—are the blocks of this communication; as Porter (1995) wrote, "numbers, too, create new things and transform the meanings of old ones" (p. 17). In order to use numbers to describe phenomena, social scientists must organize those phenomena in ways that optimize quantification (Porter, 1995). In this way, "quantification is simultaneously a means of planning and of prediction" (Porter, 1995, p. 43). Thus, social science involves considerably more human involvement in constructing quantification than even postpositivists allow.

Although postpositivism acknowledges that true objectivity is impossible to attain, there remains a belief in a modified form of objectivity that rests heavily on quantitative analysis. Of course, it is important to note here the difference between epistemology and method. Sound, rigorous research—either qualitative or quantitative—rests on coherence between theoretical framework, method, and epistemology (Smart, 2005). One can be a positivist (or postpositivist) and produce rigorous, theory-informed qualitative research. However, quantitative research is almost always from a positivist or postpositivist epistemology. Although postpositivists view quantification as a human process, true positivists persist in seeing truth reflected in numbers (Porter, 1995).

Porter (1995) tied the process of quantification to a belief in objectivity: "Social quantification means studying people in classes, abstracting away their individuality" (p. 77). Indeed, quantification is a form of power that turns "people into objects to be manipulated" (p. 77). This effect is especially felt with large data sets that people analyze with the use of statistical methods and norms (Hacking, 1992; Porter, 1995; Rose, 1990). To build samples, those who fail to conform to the norm are considered outliers and either have their experiences discarded or simply mentioned as the exception that may prove the rule (Porter, 1995). In this sense, quantification is a biopolitical technology in that it categorizes large numbers of people with an eye toward impacting the materials conditions of their lives (Foucault, 1976/1990; Luker, 2008). Obviously, this type of manipulation of large data sets is characteristic of quantitative research; by its very nature, qualitative research involves the creation of smaller samples in order to plumb the depths, rather than the contours, of a social experience.

It is this bifurcation in sampling methods that provides a clue as to how qualitative method can be a critical tool for institutional research in its ability to capture the experience of those students with marginalized identities. Postpositivists (and others) who manipulate large data sets are usually working with more or less random samples, which will ideally ensure that their data will show them the distribution of a population across categories

(Luker, 2008). These distributions will help them understand how generalizable the issue at hand may be, or, as Krathwohl (2009) put it, "what is its generality to the persons, places, times, and events beyond the situation in which it was researched" (p. 160). This urge for generalizability as well as parsimony means that, although larger, randomly sampled sets will yield more generalizable descriptions, categories judged irrelevant to the research question will inevitably be left by the wayside (Krathwohl, 2009; Luker, 2008). Thus, part of the sample creation in quantitative research involves already assuming the potential answers and relevant categories to the research question—thus leaving room for the possibility that some answers will be missed (Luker, 2008).

On the other hand, sampling methods in qualitative research are considerably more purposive (Krathwohl, 2009). Although researchers still have an idea of the questions, answers, and categories at play, there is more room for the discovery of new phenomena or experiences that may have been lost using quantitative methods. Additionally, the fact that many students who experience higher education environments in radically different ways often have marginalized identities is particularly salient—these identities make up such small proportions of larger data sets, even when oversampled, that it is difficult to make generalizable claims about their experiences. Qualitative methods provide the institutional researcher a way to not only acquire a deeper, more nuanced understanding of the experiences in their institution, but also the means to discover issues, challenges, and success that they may not have otherwise noticed. In other words, qualitative research may be one way to bridge the gap between theory's "abstraction of a few elements from the whole of human experience" and practice's "concrete and specific behaviors in complex situations" (Parker, 1977, p. 419).

Methodological Underpinnings of Issues Intelligence

To unpack the epistemological and ontological issues described above, we utilize data drawn from an exploratory qualitative study of the way that students with nonapparent disabilities experienced postsecondary learning environments (Burawoy, 1998). We defined learning environments in a manner consistent with the Hurtado, Alvarez, Guillermo-Wann, Cuellar, and Arellano (2012) Diverse Learning Environments Model, which holds that a student's specific educational experiences on a given campus arise from the confluence of societal, community, campus, and interpersonal influences. It also acknowledges the centrality of the multiple, intersecting identities of the student and those of the peers, instructors, and administrators with whom the student interacts (Hurtado et al., 2012).

Our study, which took place at a large public research university in the northeastern United States, included 18 students with nonapparent disabilities. We made the decision to focus on students with nonapparent disabilities because prior literature on the higher education experiences of students with disabilities had revealed that public perceptions of disability focused on mobility and sensory impairments (Kimball, Wells, Lauterbach, Manly, & Ostiguy, 2016). As a result, neither empirical literature nor evidence-based practice systematically addressed the experiences of people with comparatively high incidence, but nonapparent disabilities like attention deficit–hyperactivity disorder, dyslexia, and chronic medical issues (c.f., Kimball, Vaccaro, & Vargas, 2016; Vaccaro et al., 2015).

We recruited participants with a purposive sampling strategy, which sought to access students with disabilities through a recruitment email sent by the institution's disability services office. Our participants included 5 men and 13 women; 16 participants from the northeastern United States, 1 from the southern United States, and 1 international student; there were students with diverse prior schooling experiences (including public, private, and nontraditional high school experiences as well as transfer students from other community colleges and state institutions). In semistructured interviews typically ranging from 1 to 2 hours, participants were asked to describe their perceptions of the university. We also asked them to comment on their prior educational experiences. Consistent with semistructured interview protocols, these interviews varied from person to person as we followed up on unclear statements and unexpected ideas.

With the consent of the participants, we recorded all of the interviews and had them professionally transcribed. Pseudonyms were employed to ensure confidentiality. We analyzed transcribed transcripts utilizing a combination of a priori theoretical codes and emergent open codes (Burawoy, 1998; Charmaz, 2014). We then refined our analysis using several cycles of constant comparison to produce axial and thematic findings (Charmaz, 2014). Throughout our data collection and analysis process, we employed several strategies to strengthen the credibility and trustworthiness of our findings. We met regularly as a project team to address any issues and to discuss emergent findings, which functioned as a form of peer debriefing. We also utilized analytic triangulation to ensure findings were broadly representative and not the product of a single unique case. Additionally, we addressed potential issues associated with positionality by including both people with and without nonapparent disabilities on the research team and thoroughly discussing how these identities shaped our analysis. Finally, and perhaps most importantly, we remained open to new and evolving findings throughout the course of this study (Charmaz, 2014), which meant that we did not actively seek to focus on only a single type of finding.

As a result of this methodological openness, which is often a feature of qualitative research designs, we produced several unexpected findings. We describe one related to the importance of athletic participation in the section that follows. While this finding is not generalizable, which again is often a feature of qualitative research, we suggest it may well be transferable. That is, it may help to inform future analyses—both qualitative and quantitative—that seek to understand more fully the complex relationship between disability and athletic participation in the experiences of students with nonapparent disabilities.

A More Nuanced Understanding of Disability and Athletics

As noted above, the overriding public perception of disability centers on limitations—often mobility or sensory impairments—that restrict a person with a disability from participating in an activity. Often, these perceptions mean that people with disabilities are not thought of as participating in athletics (e.g., Howe, 2011; Page, O'Connor, & Peterson, 2001)—even though participation has been shown to be possible regardless of disability type (Winnick & Porretta, 2016). Our findings help to counter this perception by providing empirical evidence of the centrality of athletics to the lives of people with nonapparent disabilities. Specifically, we found that participants often described: (a) an interest in athletics as having developed as a way of "coping" with their disability when younger; (b) athletics as central to their identity and understanding of self; and (c) a complex relationship between disability, athletics, and time. One participant, Caroline, captured the interplay of these themes nicely when she described her decision to join the crew team in college:

> Actually the main reason I joined [crew] was because coming here as a fresh-man I didn't have friends yet. It was something I joined. It gave me a lot of the friends actually I have right now, which is really nice. It was also just sort of something to do. Something to give me a little bit of structure. College is totally different from high school. You make your own structure. I was kind of overwhelmed. I didn't really know what to do, how to structure my day. High school is very rigid. The bell rings then you move to the next class, bell rings and you're free. Lunch time at this specific time. I was feeling very un-organized. I didn't really know what to do with myself. Crew gave my day a lot of structure. I would see friends, I would get my workout in.

Caroline noted that the regimentation of high school had been helpful in managing the symptoms of her ADD/ADHD, which disappeared when enrolling in high school. Based on her description of the need to "get my workout in," it is also clear that athletics had long been a part of Caroline's life. Only once enrolled in college, however, did Caroline pursue crew as a mechanism for meeting people and countering her feelings of being "kind of overwhelmed" and "very unorganized." For Caroline, crew provided a mechanism for structuring her time—even while she added an additional activity to the otherwise very busy schedule of student majoring in a rigor-ous science discipline.

Athletics as "Coping" Strategy. Several participants described the importance of athletic participation in providing support and structure. A representative example is provided by Mike: "I mainly focused on my sports, and that's what kept me structured. It helped schedule my life out." For participants like Mike, the scheduled nature of individual training, practices, and competition helped to provide an order to their lives that also extended into their academics. A large part of that order stemmed from the perceived need to live up to the expectations for teammates and coaches, which several participants noted. Although this could sometimes provide a source of stress, most participants noted the positive dimension of this shared responsibility; as Francesca noted: "I always really liked doing sports. I liked that I got to have a group of people that really got to know you and like bonded together. I had sports throughout all the high schools." However, one participant with anxiety issues did note that these obligations could prove stressful as well—one of the few negative findings related to athletics in this study—when she noted that:

> Freshman year was tough for me because I was on the varsity basketball team as a freshman. I had a really bad experience with my coach and I was treated really poorly. That affected me a lot in school because I got really bad anxiety from it. I ended up quitting, which helped a lot.

Even in leaving the basketball team, however, this participant also revealed that she had learned to identify situations that were maladaptive for her success and to remove herself from them, which can be a key form of self-determination for people with disabilities (Kimball, Moore, Vaccaro, Troiano, & Newman, 2016).

Athletics and Identity.   Among our participants, it was clear that athletics served as a key way in which they understood themselves and their place in the world. In his interview, Mike described the several sports in which he participated: "I did football as a kid. I started fairly young, moved into wrestling not too long after that, and then in high school, I picked up crew. I rowed throughout high school, and I wrestled throughout high school. That's pretty much me." The statement that sports were "pretty much" him suggests that they were an integral way that he thought about himself. The comments of other participants echoed that framing. For example, Sarah noted: "I've been playing tennis since I was about 5. Which is intense. I'm not really sure what else, that's like actually who I am. I play sports and my family." Although not all participants who talked about athletics described them as related to their disability, Sarah did. She elaborated on the importance of athletic participation to her life: "That kind of goes in with the disability but, yeah I did play a variety of sports when I was younger and I kind of shifted through many different sports and tried to see which one I liked more." She elaborated on this connection a short time latter when she explained that the doctors who diagnosed her disability:

> … realized that I can see things better and I understand things when I visually see them. Whether it's directions, graphs or pictures or videos. They also said

that I would probably be very good at sports. Since I had very low self-esteem or something that I could ... that sports would probably be beneficial for me. To boost my self-esteem.

In this example, Sarah described the direct connection between her athletic participation and her self-understanding. That is, it was through athletics that she first recognized her disability to be a multivalent experience—neither wholly positive nor wholly negative.

Disability, Athletics, and Time. Although our participants described many positive attributes associated with involvement in athletics, one consistently emerged as both positive and negative: the time demands. As described above, athletics functioned for many participants as a mechanism that regulated schedules and helped establish priorities. As Caroline noted, however, she eventually had to leave crew due the extensive time commitment:

[The importance of time management] is something [my coach had] been saying since day one. I was like, you were completely right, though. It depends on who you are. Partly because of the ADD it takes me more time to do things, to get my thoughts together. Moreover just being me, I can't put this much time into a sport and also have time for my grades. It's not something I can do right now. That was the be all, end all.

Caroline describes many wonderful things about athletic participation, but the temporal demands of being a student with a disability and those associated with being a student athlete proved incompatible for her. Other participants, particularly those participating in varsity athletics, also described onerous time commitments but were able to balance them. All participants were consistent, however, in the belief that they had learned time management via athletic participation—even in Caroline's case where those same skills later helped her identify when she needed to cease her involvement.

Concluding Thoughts

As we described above, postpositivist approaches to research seek to disconfirm hypotheses intended to predict observable behavior. They hold that the role of the researcher is to mediate between the real world and observations of that world. Through methodological rigor, postpositivists argue, we can get closer to Truth—even if it remains elusive. This framing, however, requires that we have a fairly solid idea what the purpose of our inquiry is and that we have access to the methodological tools that provide us a glimpse of the underlying Truth of our area of inquiry. Sometimes neither of those things is the case.

New Directions for Institutional Research • DOI: 10.1002/ir

Our study did not set out to produce information about the athletics participation of students with nonapparent disabilities, but we did uncover potentially meaningful information about precisely that. Through qualitative interviews focused on better understanding postsecondary learning environments, participants described: (a) how athletics became a support strategy for them early in life as they learned to navigate their disability, (b) the centrality of athletics to their own self-understanding, and (c) how athletics shaped their perception of time. These are deeply personal understandings that would be difficult, if not impossible, to develop via quantitative methods or had we adopted a postpositivist approach to qualitative work. Instead, an open inquiry process consistent with constructivism (Charmaz, 2014) allowed us to remain sensitive to emerging findings. These findings, in turn, produced a deeply nuanced view of how students with nonapparent disabilities in a single institutional context made meaning of their own experiences, the diversity of the identities of student-athletes at this institution, and how we might intervene to assist students with nonapparent disabilities participating in athletics.

Additionally, they provide important information about a population of students that remains both underserved and understudied (Vaccaro et al., 2015). Existing quantitative measures of athletic participation undertaken by institutional researchers (e.g., reporting to the National Collegiate Athletic Association) do not include measures related to disability, and indeed, given federal protections related to disability status, disability status information may not even be available to institutional researchers on all campuses. Qualitative studies of this sort provide a way of gaining information about a population that might be entirely missed by attempts to quantify student experience. In so doing, they make use of the technical intelligence of institutional researchers—which includes knowing both what quantitative approaches do well and what they do poorly—to adopt alternative research approaches in order to produce information about key issues on campus.

In this case, the findings produced by our study have implications that connect the highly localized experiences of students with nonapparent disabilities to a broader literature base. As noted above, many people perceive those with disabilities to be less physically capable than those without. Our study revealed that a number of our participants with nonapparent disabilities had embraced athletics not in spite of their diagnosis but because of it, and in one case, noted that medical professionals believed them to be a better athlete because of it. As a result, our participants did not require physical accommodations to participate (Winnick & Porretta, 2016), but given concerns over time management, additional needs of temporal accommodations—that is, how to ensure that students with disabilities face the same overall time commitments as students without disabilities—would be warranted. Further, building from the observation that athletic participation had become a way of imparting structure in their lives, our findings

New Directions for Institutional Research • DOI: 10.1002/ir

suggest that interventions that use physical activity as a way to teach time management might prove helpful. Disability services offices have not historically offered this form of support (Kimball et al., 2016). Finally, our study encourages campuses to look beyond the physical dimensions of disability to acknowledge the many ways that students with disabilities engage on campus, and not to only consider their experiences when assessing disability services offices (Vaccaro et al., 2015). In short, people with disabilities are more than those disabilities, and qualitative work can help support that claim.

Ultimately, however, we must note that we do not believe this study to be exceptionally unique. While it is true that there is limited research on this topic (Kimball et al., 2016), our study provided robust information about many facets of students' experiences on campus—including their social lives, experiences in residential halls, thoughts about disability services, comments on instructor behaviors, and more. The expansive nature of constructivist qualitative work means that it will almost always produce a broader range of findings than intended: it has a way of showing the interconnectedness of otherwise disparate experiences. At the risk of overgeneralization, we believe that observation to be transferable well beyond the population that we used to produce it. That is, although we focused on students with disabilities, we believe the utility of qualitative methods to hold true for any minoritized, marginalized, or historically underrepresented student population. In these cases, qualitative methods can go well beyond what is true for most students and get at the individual stories that comprise (and often vary from) the general pattern.

References

Burawoy, M. (1998). The extended case method. *Sociological Theory, 16*(1), 4–33.

Charmaz, K. (2014). Constructing grounded theory: A practical guide through qualitative analysis (2nd ed.). Thousand Oaks, CA: Sage.

Faircloth, S. C., Alcantar, C. M., & Stage, F. K. (2015). Use of large-scale data sets to study educational pathways of American Indian and Alaska Native students. *New Directions for Institutional Research, 2014*(163), 5–24.

Foucault, M. (1990). *The history of sexuality: Volume 1: An introduction* (R. Hurley, Trans.). New York, NY: Vintage Books. (Original work published 1976).

Hacking, I. (1992). Statistical language, statistical truth, and statistical reason: The self-authentication of a style of scientific reasoning. In E. McMullin (Ed.), *The social dimensions of science* (pp. 130–157). Notre Dame, IN: University of Notre Dame Press.

Howe, P. D. (2011). Cyborg and supercrip: The Paralympics technology and the (dis)empowerment of disabled athletes. *Sociology, 45*(5), 868–882.

Hurtado, S., Alvarez, C. L., Guillermo-Wann, C., Cuellar, M., & Arellano, L. (2012). A model for diverse learning environments. In J. C. Smart & M. B. Paulsen (Eds.), *Higher education: Handbook of theory and research* (pp. 41–122). New York, NY: Springer.

Kimball, E., Moore, A., Vaccaro, A., Troiano, P., & Newman, B. (2016). College students with disabilities redefine activism: Self-advocacy, storytelling, and collective action. *Journal of Diversity in Higher Education, 9*(3), 245–260.

Kimball, E., Wells, R. S., Lauterbach, A., Manly, C., & Ostiguy, B. (2016). Students with disabilities in higher education: A review of the literature and an agenda for future research. In *Higher education: Handbook of theory and research*. Dordrecht, Netherlands: Springer.

Kimball, E. W., Vaccaro, A., & Vargas, N. (2016). Student affairs professionals supporting students with disabilities: A grounded theory model. *Journal of Student Affairs Research & Practice, 53*(2), 175–189.

Krathwohl, D. R. (2009). *Methods of educational and social science research: The logic of methods* (3rd ed.). Long Grove, IL: Waveland Press.

Kuhn, T. S. (1977). *The essential tension: Selected studies in scientific tradition and change.* Chicago, IL: University of Chicago Press.

Lagemann, E. C. (2002). *An elusive science: The troubling history of education research.* Chicago, IL: University of Chicago Press.

Luker, K. (2008). *Salsa dancing into the social sciences: Research in an age of info-glut.* Cambridge, MA: Harvard University Press.

Page, S. J., O'Connor, E., & Peterson, K. (2001). Leaving the disability ghetto: A qualitative study of factors underlying achievement motivation among athletes with disabilities. *Journal of Sport & Social Issues, 25*(1), 40–55.

Parker, C. A. (1977). On modeling reality. *Journal of College Student Personnel, 18*, 419–425.

Popper, K. (2002). *The logic of scientific discovery.* New York, NY: Routledge. (Original work published 1935).

Porter, T. M. (1995). *Trust in numbers: The pursuit of objectivity in science and public life.* Princeton, NJ: Princeton University Press.

Rose, N. (1990). *Governing the soul.* London, United Kingdom: Routledge.

Smart, J. C. (2005). Perspectives of the editor: Attributes of exemplary research manuscripts employing quantitative analyses. *Research in Higher Education, 46*(4), 461–477.

Taleb, N. N. (2007). *The black swan: The impact of the highly improbable.* New York, NY: Random House.

Vaccaro, A., Kimball, E., Ostiguy, B., & Wells, R. S. (2015). Researching students with disabilities: The importance of critical perspectives. *New Directions for Institutional Research, 163*, 25–41.

Winnick, J., & Porretta, D. (Eds.). (2016). *Adapted Physical Education and Sport, 6E.* Champaign, IL: Human Kinetics.

RACHEL E. FRIEDENSEN *is a postdoctoral researcher at Iowa State University.*

BYRON P. MCCRAE *is the vice president of Student Life & dean of students at Davidson College.*

EZEKIEL KIMBALL *is an assistant professor of higher education at the University of Massachusetts Amherst.*

5

This chapter describes efforts to gather and utilize qualitative data to maximize contextual knowledge at one university. The examples provided focus on how academic departments use qualitative evidence to enhance their students' success as well as how qualitative evidence supports the institution's broader strategic planning goals.

Context Matters: Using Qualitative Inquiry to Inform Departmental Effectiveness and Student Success

Elizabeth A. Williams, Martha L.A. Stassen

The dominance of quantitative inquiry within the field of higher education both historically and currently is indisputable. Quantitative analysis of institutional data and survey data typifies most research produced for institutional decision-making as well as studies published in the field's top journals—both of which contribute to the development of organizational intelligence for higher education institutions (Terenzini, 1993, 2013). Although many prominent higher education researchers have emphasized the merits of qualitative inquiry over the past few decades, quantitative research remains the stock-in-trade for most institutional research and assessment professionals.

A decade ago, Harper and Kuh (2007) chided institutional researchers for eschewing qualitative methods and valuing "the general" more than "the specific" (p. 5). They observed that institutional researchers purposefully steer away from qualitative methods because of numerous, shared "misconceptions" about the value, utility, and trustworthiness of qualitative data. Concurrently, Chism and Banta (2007) offered a somewhat contrasting perspective, pointing to changing norms and increased reliance on qualitative inquiry in assessment activities. They highlighted a variety of ways that institutional researchers have employed qualitative methods to assess a broad array of institutional aspects, including course effectiveness, general education goals, student support services, and overall institutional effectiveness.

The Office of Academic Planning and Assessment (OAPA) at the University of Massachusetts Amherst coordinates external Student Learning

New Directions for Institutional Research, no. 174 © 2017 Wiley Periodicals, Inc.
Published online in Wiley Online Library (wileyonlinelibrary.com) • DOI: 10.1002/ir.20221

Assessment requirements for the University and works with Academic Affairs departments and other units on campus-wide student learning and experience assessment activities, including curricular assessment for General Education and consultation with academic departments on their own assessment and program review activities. OAPA also directs other campus-wide evaluation and assessment projects for the University (e.g., our recent Campus Climate Survey). As a part of our work supporting department and campus-wide assessment, we conduct substantial research into the quality of the undergraduate and graduate student experience, both inside and outside the classroom and academic curriculum. Qualitative evidence is a cornerstone of our efforts to enhance contextual awareness and diminish the possibility of "intelligence failure" (Fincher, 1978) in these and other areas of research. Deep, rich, contextual intelligence can help administrators and faculty answer complex questions and facilitate their ability to harness quantitative data effectively to develop policies and practices that promote positive outcomes for students. In this chapter, we describe our efforts to gather and utilize qualitative data to maximize contextual knowledge and promote "a culture of evidence" in accordance with our university's strategic plan (University of Massachusetts Amherst Joint Task Force on Strategic Oversight, 2013, p. 6). The examples we provide focus specifically on how academic departments use qualitative evidence to enhance their students' success as well as how qualitative evidence supports broader University strategic planning goals.

Perspectives on Methodological Pluralism

Recognition and critique of the predominance of quantitative inquiry within the field of higher education is longstanding. Keller's (1998) treatise warned against "methodological monism" and advocated for "pluralism" in the research methods used to develop knowledge to inform higher education policy and practice (p. 268). Keller emphasized that "understanding is gained by doing the utmost with whatever tools work best, no holds barred, to describe, analyze, and suggest improved designs for academic institutions and their activities" (p. 275). Yet, despite well-reasoned pleas by Keller and others, quantitative inquiry's hold on higher education scholars and institutional researchers has remained firm. Studies published in the field's top-tier journals are primarily quantitative (Hutchinson & Lovell, 2004), with a recent investigation showing no evidence of increased diversity in the methods that published researchers employed to generate knowledge about higher education (Wells, Kolek, Williams, & Saunders, 2015). *Research in Higher Education*, which was until recently the *Journal of the Association for Institutional Research*, is the most quantitatively oriented of these top journals and boasts the largest publication volume. This lay of the land suggests that the coaching Harper and Kuh (2007) offered to institutional researchers to encourage adjusted methodological mindsets also

New Directions for Institutional Research • DOI: 10.1002/ir

should be extended to higher education scholars given their influential roles as publication gatekeepers, mentors, and shapers of the field.

Whether or not the quantitative hold on higher education researchers is attributable to widespread misunderstandings about qualitative research, the benefits of qualitative inquiry have been recognized and promoted within the field for as long as "methodological monism" has been critiqued. Twenty-five years ago, Terenzini and Pascarella (1991) shared a set of research lessons drawn from their comprehensive analysis of 20 years of college impact studies. One of these suggestions was, "Greater use should be made of qualitative research methods" (p. 89). Pointing to the predominantly quantitative nature of research on college impact, Terenzini and Pascarella emphasized the value of qualitative approaches for "providing greater sensitivity to many of the subtle and fine-grained complexities" (p. 89).

Since Terenzini and Pascarella (1991) shared their insights about the value of qualitative inquiry, several researchers have advocated for harnessing qualitative methods to gather contextual data to complement the quantitative data relied on so extensively by colleges and universities in the quest for organizational intelligence. Hathaway (1995) argued that using quantitative and qualitative data in tandem—rather than quantitative data solely—facilitates understanding of "what is going on" (p. 555). Borland (2001) also emphasized the complementarity of quantitative and qualitative methods, and pointed to qualitative research as "the only means" to provide campus leaders with "data that is contextually and humanly framed" (p. 8). Perkins (2001) similarly advocated for using both quantitative and qualitative methods to provide a "rich" context for institutional decision-making. Kroc and Hanson (2003) included qualitative research methods in the skill set recommended to institutional researchers engaged in enrollment management studies, pointing to the power of qualitative research to offer "insights that will otherwise be missed" (p. 91).

Deeper Insights Into Departmental Effectiveness and Student Success

Like similar operations at other universities, UMass Amherst's OAPA provides academic departments and the University administration with a wealth of quantitative information about the nature and quality of the undergraduate student experience. This body of evidence includes an annual Senior Survey, data from the National Survey of Student Engagement (NSSE) (done every 3 years), Student Response to Instruction (course evaluation) data, an Alumni Survey, an Advising Experiences Survey, and surveys specific to our First-Year Seminars and upper-division "Integrative Experience" General Education requirement. To the greatest extent possible, we disaggregate our survey data by academic department to provide faculty and administrators with insights into where their students' experiences are particularly positive and where causes for concern and attention lie. Student ratings are arrayed from high to low across departments with indications of which departmental scores are a standard deviation above or below the campus mean. Yet, as extensive as this quantitative evidence is, Deans, department chairs, and faculty routinely ask, "But what do these survey results mean? Why are students saying this/rating us this way? What should we do to improve?"

These reasonable questions beg answers, of course. Particularly when campus leadership is asking departments and faculty members to assess their strengths and areas for improvement and take actions to enhance the student experience. Because "the best decisions are based on a deeper understanding than quantitative methods alone can provide" (Chism & Banta, 2007, p. 15), we incorporate a healthy dose of qualitative inquiry into our assessment activities. Qualitative evidence is a cornerstone of our efforts to provide contextual intelligence that can help administrators and faculty develop answers to complex questions—and facilitate their ability to utilize the abundance of quantitative data available to them effectively. Our efforts to gather and utilize qualitative data, which we describe here, are three-pronged: (a) routine use of open-ended survey questions, (b) in-depth department and campus-wide qualitative inquiry, and (c) intentional dissemination of research findings.

Qualitative Inquiry for Contextual Intelligence

Routine Use of Open-Ended Survey Questions.   Survey research is a mainstay of our assessment operation and we rely on both prominent, national surveys and surveys we develop in-house. We use many of these survey data sets to create campus-wide snapshots of the "overall" undergraduate student experience. The CIRP Freshman Survey and NSSE also offer national benchmarks that allow us to compare our students and their experiences to those of other similar institutions. However, perhaps the most effective use of survey data for informing institutional practices and directing change efforts derives from our emphasis on department-level analyses and reporting of results (and, when numbers do not allow, school/college level results). As described earlier, the quantitative data we distribute provide departments with indicators of where their students' experiences are particularly high or low. But Deans, department heads and chairs, and faculty often have trouble translating the aggregate results into action. This is where our qualitative data analyses and reporting are essential. Here, we describe three instances of providing qualitative survey results (in conjunction with quantitative survey results) to departments and instructors to inform departmental action.

Senior Survey.   Each spring semester, OAPA conducts a Senior Survey to gather data about graduating seniors' overall experience at the University. Because this survey typically achieves a response rate of 70% or more,

NEW DIRECTIONS FOR INSTITUTIONAL RESEARCH • DOI: 10.1002/ir

the data can be used at the department level. The survey asks graduating seniors to report on their level of satisfaction with particular aspects of their major (e.g., access to classes, quality of teaching, accessibility of faculty, academic advising); participation in high-impact activities; perceived learning outcomes; and postgraduation employment and/or graduate school plans. The part of the survey focused on students' experience in their major includes the following open-ended question: "Please provide specific feedback to your department on how your experience in your major could have been improved."

Roughly one-half of survey participants across more than 50 academic majors/programs respond to this question. Drawing from students' responses over a number of years of survey administration, OAPA has developed a set of codes that organizes students' comments into broad categories (e.g., advising, faculty/teaching) with subcodes that provide the specific types of responses in these broad categories (e.g., under advising the subcodes include "better academic advising or support" and "better career advising/planning"). This inductive approach to developing codes, whereby we review students' responses and build the broad categories and subthemes based on those responses, guides most of our qualitative analyses and reporting. OAPA staff members code the senior survey responses with the use of the coding scheme we have developed and sort the results by major. In addition to department-specific and comparative quantitative results from the survey, each department receives the complete set of verbatim open-ended responses, along with the OAPA's coding of those responses. Our coding of graduating seniors' comments helps departments understand the major themes emerging in their students' responses, whereas students' own words provide the color and texture of those responses. OAPA's precoding of student responses is particularly helpful for large departments and majors where making systematic sense of numerous student responses can be challenging and time consuming. For all departments, the open-ended comments can assist with sense-making about the quantitative survey results, and provide insight into specific program aspects that students recognize to be obstacles or barriers to their success.

In recent years, as the University's strategic planning efforts have asked all departments to engage in unit planning efforts focused on the quality of their undergraduate students' experiences, these qualitative results have become even more important because they provide departments with specific suggestions and areas for improvement. Departments were tasked with reviewing the evidence available to them about their students' experiences and using this information to identify strengths, areas for improvement, and next steps for enhancing the undergraduate experience. By request of the Deans and several departments, OAPA provided departments with 5 years' worth of coded and quantitatively summarized open-ended Senior Survey responses (see Figure 5.1). Used in conjunction with a wide array of quantitative data, these qualitative data helped departments identify long-term

Figure 5.1. Coded and quantitatively summarized open-ended senior survey responses.

UMass Amherst GRADUATING SENIOR SURVEY OPEN-ENDED FEEDBACK

Please provide specific feedback to your department about how your experience in your major could have been improved.*

Number who responded by comment category and year of survey

Verbatim comments and coding, by year, are available in additional tabs.

SAMPLE DEPARTMENT	Comment Category	2012	2013	2014	2015	2016	All Years Total	Percent
COURSES	Smaller class sizes	2	5	5	2	0	14	3%
	Better course availability and access	34	37	15	6	6	98	23%
	More variety; suggestions for other course topics	2	5	0	0	3	10	2%
	Improved course content, difficulty, or quality	1	0	2	3	3	9	2%
	Need more practical and hands-on experience	0	5	3	2	7	17	4%
	Other comments on courses	2	2	2	1	5	12	3%
FACULTY/TEACHING	Better faculty accessibility and concern	3	4	0	2	3	12	3%
	Need more faculty or staff, fewer TAs	10	2	2	1	0	15	4%
	Improve quality of teaching	0	0	3	2	1	6	1%
	Other comments on faculty	0	1	2	1	0	4	1%
MAJOR/DEPARTMENT	Better organization, emphasis on a certain field; add concentration	1	6	4	5	4	20	5%
	Department concern, communication, or community	1	1	0	1	1	4	1%
	Better facilities, equipment, or computers/technology	2	2	4	1	5	14	3%
	Other comments on the major or department	1	2	3	4	6	16	4%
ADVISING	Better academic advising or support	7	10	12	14	14	57	13%
	Better career advising/planning	5	7	11	8	14	45	11%
POSTIVE OR NO COMMENT	Positive comments on the major	6	12	14	16	15	63	15%
	Nothing, no improvements needed	0	3	1	2	0	6	1%
OTHER	All other comments	0	1	0	4	1	6	1%
TOTALS	TOTAL WHO ANSWERED ITEM	77	105	83	75	88	428	100%
	TOTAL SURVEY RESPONDENTS	160	189	192	197	172	910	
	PERCENT WHO ANSWERED ITEM	48%	56%	43%	38%	51%	47%	

*Item wording changed in 2016. The 2012-2015 wording was "Please give feedback to your department on how your experience in your major could have been improved."

trends in students' recommendations and establish priorities for action. The open-ended responses from the Senior Survey have also proved essential for informing institution-wide changes to undergraduate advising structures and priorities across campus. Advising is among the most mentioned area for needed improvement, and graduating seniors' insights have been influential in shaping advising priorities and strategies across departments and colleges/schools.

General Education Survey.   In 2012, the University capped off a multiyear review of its General Education (Gen Ed) program by instituting an upper-division Integrative Experience (IE) general education requirement. As a part of the ongoing assessment of this new requirement, OAPA administers a course experience survey each semester to all students enrolled in an IE. The results of this survey are shared with IE instructors to inform their ongoing course improvements and with department heads and chairs to inform departments' overall approaches to the requirement. The aggregate survey results are also shared with the Faculty Senate Gen Ed Council (a faculty senate group comprised of faculty, students, and administrators) as a part of their ongoing review of the effectiveness of the new program requirement.

We have also used this particular survey as an opportunity to explore other, broader questions associated with Gen Ed. In Fall 2015, we used the survey to inform ongoing discussions about the possibility of offering a theme-based approach to Gen Ed. We asked survey participants about their level of interest in such an approach, and to offer recommendations for possible themes.

The IE survey garnered a 60% response rate and over 35% of students responded to the open-ended request for possible Gen Ed themes. We coded and analyzed survey participants' recommendations, and created a visual illustrating the clusters and frequencies of these suggested themes (see Figure 5.2). This information was shared with the Gen Ed Council and the Vice Provost for Undergraduate Education to inform their ongoing consideration of improvements to the Gen Ed curriculum. Although campus Gen Ed priorities have taken the curricular discussion in other directions for the time being, the affirmation of student interest in curricular themes, and the wealth of ideas emerging from them, have provided important guidance for future Gen Ed reform efforts. Perhaps more immediately relevant, this approach to collecting guidance on curricular reform from the student perspective has proven to be valuable and enlightening, and is a strategy we will certainly use in future curricular investigations.

Student Learning Survey.   One final example of our use of open-ended survey questions is the Student Learning Survey, a project initiated and pursued by the Innovative Pedagogy Assessment Group (InPAG)—a working group assembled by University administrators and collaboratively led by OAPA and the Center for Teaching and Faculty Development (now the Institute for Teaching Excellence & Faculty Development). UMass Amherst's

Figure 5.2. A visual illustration of the clusters and frequencies of suggested Gen Ed themes.

2015 IE Student Survey - New Item - General Education Clusters

The University is considering establishing thematic "clusters" of Gen Ed courses that students could use to guide their Gen Ed course selections. Students could select courses that address a common theme or interest, such as "Sustainability," "Technology and Social Change," or "The Visual World," to design a more integrated and personalized Gen Ed curriculum.

If thematic clusters had existed when you planned your own Gen Eds, would you have chosen to pursue courses linked by a common theme?

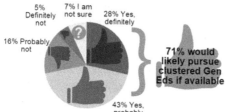

5% Definitely not

7% I am not sure

28% Yes, definitely

16% Probably not

43% Yes, probably

71% would likely pursue clustered Gen Eds if available

Please provide any suggestions you have for topics or themes that you think would be of interest to you and your peers. In addition, please use this space to provide any other suggestions or comments about the Gen Ed "cluster" idea.

Office of Academic Planning & Assessment
June 2015

strategic plan highlights active learning as the "centerpiece" of University efforts to improve undergraduate education. The Student Learning Survey was designed and conducted to explore students' experiences in courses taught by faculty known to have adopted active learning strategies, including the expanded array of Team-Based Learning (TBL) courses held (primarily) in the University's new Integrative Learning Center. InPAG identified an emerging need for data pertaining to pedagogical innovation and active learning experiences on our campus, including self-report data from students about their course experiences.

To meet this data need, OAPA developed (in consultation with InPAG) the Student Learning Survey and Student Learning Follow-Up Survey, the first being a "Time 1" survey administered on the first day of class, and the second being a "Time 2" survey administered near the end of the semester. In Fall 2015, we administered the paper, scannable surveys in-class to more than 1,800 students in 10 different TBL courses and we achieved a matched response rate of 50% or more for 6 of the 10 courses. The Time 2 survey included a closed-response question that asked students to rate their learning experience in the course on a scale ranging from *Poor* to *Excellent*. To understand the reasons underlying students' ratings, we included this follow-up open-ended question: "Please provide any additional information that would help us understand your overall rating of your learning experience."

OAPA coded students' responses to this question both within and across courses. Overall, the open-ended question elicited an array of both negative and positive feedback. The dominant negative themes were the challenges of designing effective group work, poor teaching, perceived inappropriateness of the TBL format for the course, and a dislike of the TBL format in general. Dominant positive themes included perceived benefits of teamwork, excellent teaching, and an affinity for the TBL course format in general. We provided the course-level open-ended comments and accompanying codes to instructors for their own use in further developing and enhancing their TBL courses and, in the aggregate, to the instructional development office to inform their support of the TBL efforts. The aggregate set of open-ended responses offered substantial insight to campus administrators and faculty about both the substantial challenges and promising opportunities associated with teaching for active learning.

The three examples of OAPA's use of open-ended survey questions discussed here relate to surveys developed in-house. But for our recent NSSE administration, we embraced the option to include a concluding, open-ended question. We chose a question that asks students to identify the "most satisfying" and "most disappointing" aspects of their experience at the University. Because we achieved a response rate of nearly 50%, we anticipate that our forthcoming NSSE data set will include a substantial set of rich comments that offer a wide range of insights about first-year students' and seniors' experiences. Although NSSE's primary focus is students' academic experiences, the broad wording of this open-ended question leaves the door open for students to consider and comment on their university experience holistically. We look forward to sharing these qualitative data with our partners in academic affairs and student affairs alike.

In-Depth Qualitative Inquiry with Academic Partners. The qualitative inquiry and coding of survey responses described above provide departments and academic leadership with more clarity about the student experience than the quantitative survey results alone can offer. However, this information is sometimes more of a "teaser" than completely revelatory of how departments should proceed to improve their performance. The administration's unit planning focus, which asks departments to review available evidence and identify strengths and areas for improvement, has sparked increased departmental interest in deeper and richer insights into their students' experiences.

Department-Based Focus Groups. Although OAPA has always offered departments the opportunity to work with us to conduct focus groups of their student majors, departmental requests for this service have escalated under the new strategic planning prioritization of evidence-informed departmental action to improve the undergraduate experience. Upon departmental college/school request, we have conducted focus groups for both "stand-alone" academic departments, and a set of departments within a particular college/school. Having worked with some of the initial departments to develop a focus-group protocol that covered the issues of interest to them, we now have a standard focus-group protocol template that we invite departments to adjust as they see fit. The questions included in the template focus primarily on undergraduate priorities identified in the campus-wide strategic plan (e.g., student engagement and active learning, advising and career support, curricular coherence, progress on learning objectives). The focus groups we conduct typically address three to four main topics, and we plan for focus group discussions that last from 60 to 75 minutes.

OAPA staff members conduct the focus groups and we assure the confidentiality of students' responses. We recommend this practice over members of the department themselves conducting the focus group sessions to facilitate students' candid responses about their experiences in the major. We record the sessions digitally and analyze the conversation to identify primary themes, important insights, and compelling quotes, synthesizing the findings in a report we provide to the department. Although departments sometimes express an interest in receiving a transcript of the focus group conversation, we have not been able to accommodate all such requests due to resource limitations. When we have provided transcripts, we have taken great care to mask students' identities to ensure the high level of confidentiality we promised.

The results of the focus groups provide deeper and more specific insights to departments about how to shape their priorities for their undergraduates' experiences. As we conduct these focus groups, we frequently are struck by the creative and well-grounded recommendations and specific

NEW DIRECTIONS FOR INSTITUTIONAL RESEARCH • DOI: 10.1002/ir

suggestions students provide. Often, they brainstorm together how their department could realistically improve a given challenge. The enthusiasm they demonstrate in these discussions illustrates how much they appreciate being asked for their input.

Departments have used the information we provide to help develop and refine their advising strategies, consider curricular changes to provide greater opportunities for students to interact with each other and with departmental faculty, and to convince reluctant faculty colleagues about the importance of developing career guidance or other interventions for student success. For example, in focus groups for a large department overwhelmed with increasing numbers of majors, students consistently expressed a desire for more contact with faculty. Although they acknowledge that their faculty are inspiring role models in the discipline, students perceived that many faculty seemed more interested in their research than in undergraduates. These students also described a sense of alienation from their major during the first two years of study. The department chair used this information to foster faculty conversations about how to achieve increased faculty–student interactions in the early years of students' experiences and created an undergraduate student advisory board to facilitate ongoing student–faculty interaction and student feedback. Although this department's quantitative Senior Survey data had, for years, indicated a lack of satisfaction with student–faculty interaction, this could be explained away by the large number of students and need for more faculty lines. However, hearing students' appreciation for the expertise of their instructors and their hunger for greater opportunities to interact moved the Chair and other faculty members to develop creative ways to build better interactions, even as they pursued possibilities of additional faculty positions.

General Education and Campus Experience Focus Groups.   The confluence of the strategic planning goal to make UMass Amherst a destination of choice for undergraduates and the assessment of a new General Education requirement provided a perfect opportunity to expand our focus-group–based qualitative inquiry to address campus-wide priorities as well as department-specific needs. With funding support from the Davis Educational Foundation (provided to help the University with the implementation and evaluation of our new Integrative Experience [IE] general education requirement), we conducted a series of nine focus groups, three each with sophomores, juniors, and seniors. This focus-group project, unprecedented in its extensiveness and range of scope, investigated the following main topics: overall positive and negative aspects of students' UMass experience, experiences with integrative and reflective learning (tied to the IE/General Education curricular assessment), and the characteristics and student experiences that make the UMass experience distinctive.

We recruited focus-group participants by sending email invitations to random samples of students, sometimes sending a second wave of invites to an additional sample to ensure optimal group size (8–10 students per group). We held the focus groups in the late afternoon in a private conference room in the Chancellor's and Provost's joint administrative suite, both because of its central campus location and its symbolic underscoring of the importance of the research. As student participants arrived at the conference room, we asked them to engage in a brief, individual mapping exercise whereby they contemplated, and then sketched out on a worksheet, possible connections among their various University experiences up to that point. This prefocus group reflective activity helped prime students for some of the focus-group questions pertaining to integrative educational experiences.

Anticipating that the focus groups would yield valuable information about the undergraduate experience, we invited one of our student affairs partners to sit in on the conversations. Thanks to the generous and articulate sharing of personal experiences and perspectives on the part of our participants, the focus groups did not disappoint: The conversations were jam-packed with insights. We did not anticipate, but were delighted, that so many of the students expressed appreciation for the focus-group opportunity. We recorded and transcribed the focus-group conversations and analyzed the results with the use of NVivo™ qualitative analyses software. The results have informed the ongoing development of the IE curriculum as well as General Education unit planning more broadly. They have also been used to inform institution-wide strategies for student success, as is described in the next section about use and reporting of qualitative results.

Intentional Dissemination of Research Findings.   As seasoned institutional research and assessment professionals are aware, the challenge of fostering and supporting organizational intelligence encompasses not only gathering, organizing, and analyzing data, but effective communication and dissemination of research findings (Volkwein, 2010). Promoting general awareness of the array of data available and alerting campus colleagues about new research results in a timely fashion are key aspects of our mission. Data and research results can fuel organizational intelligence only when they are accessed and engaged with by decision makers and their influencers. Ideally, it would be second nature for administrators and others to seek out data and research results immediately upon encountering a problem or administrative challenge—and for many, it is. But fostering and helping to sustain a "culture of evidence," one of the main tenets of our university's strategic plan, calls for concerted action. To this end, we organized a Joint Meeting on Student Success workshop to develop campuswide awareness of available information, share findings of recent OAPA research endeavors, facilitate use of these findings to inform student success initiatives, and spark the development of "unified" initiatives (University of Massachusetts Amherst Joint Task Force on Strategic Oversight, 2013, p. 18) to enhance the undergraduate experience.

The half-day Joint Meeting on Student Success was attended by approximately 50 student success coordinators, assessment coordinators, and undergraduate deans, from both academic and student affairs. The workshop included a multi-part, Prezi™-facilitated presentation by a team of five OAPA staff members, as well as facilitated small-group activities. The presentation featured findings drawn from six specific data sources, including three of those discussed here in this chapter. Although our presentation included quantitative findings from the CIRP Freshman Survey (one of the "takeaways" we provided in participants' workshop packets was an infographic tailored to their college/school or other work-unit), knowledge gained through our qualitative inquiries took center stage. The workshop provided an opportunity for us to showcase a few of the one-page visual depictions carefully developed to facilitate effective dissemination of our qualitative research findings. One of these was a pair of word clouds depicting the positive and negative words/phrases that focus group participants used to describe their undergraduate experience so far, whereas the other was a visual mapping of students' positive and negative assessments of the general education curriculum (see Figure 5.3). We included both visuals in participants' takeaway packets.

Our workshop presentation included a generous selection of compelling data from our focus-group projects—students' own words describing their experiences, perceptions of, and reflections on their undergraduate experience. These personal expressions described the challenges of finding a "path," feelings of excitement and enlightenment, pressures of unrelenting decision-making, struggles to make connections, adjusting to looking out for one's self, and longing for caring and interested advisors and faculty. Students' voices resonated powerfully with workshop participants, underscoring the emotionally compelling nature of first-hand accounts.

Not surprisingly, we asked workshop participants to complete a brief, anonymous workshop evaluation form, which the vast majority completed. Nearly all participants (98%) indicated that the workshop was very or somewhat useful to their work, which validated our efforts. Several participants suggested having additional Joint Meetings to facilitate collaboration as well as having "data days" to facilitate better integration and dissemination of available data related to student success. Participants' positive reactions convinced us that the Joint Meeting was a worthwhile and engaging endeavor worth repeating annually, or even each semester.

Conclusion

The tool chest of quantitative analysis is, of course, fundamental to our institutional research and assessment work. It is essential that we help members of the University community get beyond anecdotes and personal experiences to understand aggregate pictures and how results compare across groups, departments, and institutions. At the same time, inviting written expression and explanation, listening to participants' voices, creating visual representations of texts and voices to aid understanding—

Figure 5.3. One-page visual depictions developed to facilitate effective dissemination of qualitative research findings.

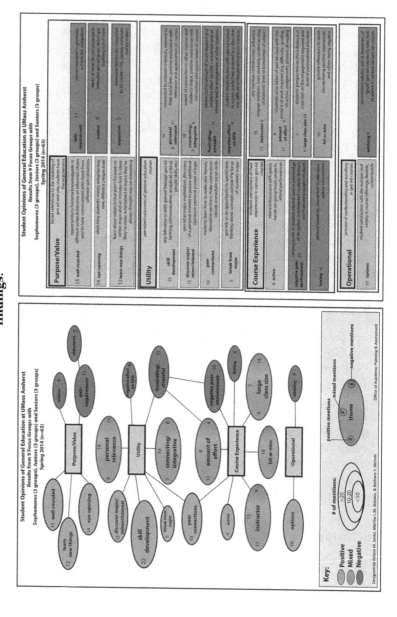

these qualitative methods offer the texture and context that make the quantitative and systematic evidence come alive. Together they represent our pluralistic approach to institutional assessment.

As evidenced by the examples provided here, this synergistic approach—considering qualitative and quantitative data in tandem—is superior to quantitative-only approaches for facilitating institutional, administrative, departmental, and instructor change and improvement. In their book *Switch: How to Change Things When Change is Hard* (Heath & Heath, 2011), the authors describe how change is more likely to occur when both the rational and emotional sides of our brains are activated. The rational side (full of analysis and deliberation) provides the planning and direction for action, and the emotional side (where compassion, sympathy, and loyalty are evidenced) provides the energy or motivation to act. In many ways, we have found that our quantitative analyses and bar charts are good at activating rational and deliberative thought and prompting questions or requests for additional information. Often, however, it is the student voices—whether the immediacy of a compelling personal account or a crisply formed frustration or recommendation—that energizes departmental action and convinces skeptics that action is needed. This is, of course, not a perfect analogy—quantitative results can excite empathy; a thoughtful story can lead to deliberative and analytic thought. The point, however, is clear: Compelling evidence is multifaceted and activates various parts of our brains for action.

Also, and somewhat selfishly, we integrate qualitative inquiry into our assessment efforts because doing so adds value to our own work and professional development as researchers. Collecting and analyzing qualitative evidence brings us into personal contact with students—both through reading and analyzing their responses to open-ended survey questions and through communicating directly with them in focus groups or interviews. Because much of our time as institutional researchers is spent sitting at computers analyzing data, or talking with colleagues, administrators, or faculty members, it is too easy for us to become far removed from undergraduates' day-to-day experiences on our campus. Without question the outcomes of our qualitative inquiry facilitate the contextual understandings upon which successful strategic planning and change actions depend. In addition, the inquiry processes themselves help us to connect with and understand students —the most fundamental of our constituents—in invaluable ways.

References

Borland, K. W., Jr. (2001). Qualitative and quantitative research: A complementary balance. *New Directions for Institutional Research, 112,* 5–13.

Chism, N., & Banta, T. W. (2007). Enhancing institutional assessment efforts through qualitative methods. *New Directions for Institutional Research, 136,* 15–28.

Fincher, C. (1978). Institutional research as organizational intelligence. *Research in Higher Education, 8*(2), 189–192.

Harper, S. R., & Kuh, G. D. (2007). Myths and misconceptions about using qualitative methods in assessment. *New Directions for Institutional Research, 136,* 5–14.

Hathaway, R. S. (1995). Assumptions underlying quantitative and qualitative research: Implications for institutional research. *Research in Higher Education, 36*(5), 535–562.

Heath, C., & Heath, D. (2011). *Switch: How to change things when change is hard.* New York, NY: Random House Books.

Hutchinson, S., & Lovell, C. (2004). A review of methodological characteristics of research published in key journals in higher education: Implications for graduate research training. *Research in Higher Education, 45*(4), 383–403.

Keller, G. (1998). Does higher education research need revisions? *Review of Higher Education, 21*(3), 267–276.

Kroc, R. J., & Hanson, G. (2003). Enrollment management. In W. E. Knight (Ed.), *Resources in Institutional Research, No. 14. The Primer for Institutional Research* (pp. 79–102). Tallahassee, FL: The Association for Institutional Research.

Perkins, M. L. (2001). The use of quantitative and qualitative information in institutional decision making. *New Directions for Institutional Research, 112,* 85–95.

Terenzini, P. T. (1993). On the nature of institutional research and the knowledge and skills it requires. *Research in Higher Education, 34*(1), 1–10.

Terenzini, P. T. (2013). "On the nature of institutional research" revisited: Plus ça change…? *Research in Higher Education, 54*(2), 137–148.

Terenzini, P. T., & Pascarella, E. T. (1991). Twenty years of research on college students: Lessons for future research. *Research in Higher Education, 32*(1), 83–92.

University of Massachusetts Amherst Joint Task Force on Strategic Oversight. (2013). *Innovation and impact: Renewing the promise of the public research university.* Amherst, MA: Author.

Volkwein, J. F. (2010). Reporting research results effectively. *New Directions for Institutional Research, 2010*(S1), 155–163.

Wells, R. S., Kolek, E. A., Williams, E. A., & Saunders, D. B. (2015). "How we know what we know:" A systematic comparison of research methods employed in higher education journals, 1996–2000 v. 2006–2010. *The Journal of Higher Education, 86*(2), 171–198.

ELIZABETH A. WILLIAMS *is director of Survey and Evaluation Research in the Office of Academic Planning and Assessment and an adjunct faculty member in Higher Education at the University of Massachusetts Amherst.*

MARTHA L. A. STASSEN *is an associate provost for Assessment and Educational Effectiveness and director of the Office of Academic Planning and Assessment at the University of Massachusetts Amherst.*

NEW DIRECTIONS FOR INSTITUTIONAL RESEARCH • DOI: 10.1002/ir

This chapter provides a conceptual model that institutional research professionals can use to develop contextual intelligence of issues of interest in higher education with the use of case studies from peer institutions. The model draws from the metaphor of the "divided brain" and how the two hemispheres must work together with both broad and focused attention on an issue grounded in contextual understanding.

Cooperative Attention: Using Qualitative Case Studies to Study Peer Institutions

Bethany Lisi

There are many opportunities for institutional research (IR) professionals to develop their technical and issues intelligence through their on-the-job work, particularly in creating and administering internal surveys to learn more about an issue on campus, or through external accountability demands such as IPEDS or accreditation self-studies. Each new data event, for instance, conducting focus-group interviews or document analysis, offers opportunities for IR professionals to grow their methodological toolkit and understanding of the problems administrators confront at their institutions. Both technical and issues intelligence use a procedural or process-oriented lens to conduct the work (Terenzini, 2013). Developing contextual intelligence, which is harder to master, requires a different kind of lens—a more mindful awareness of what is happening within the confines of the institution and in the larger ecology of higher education. In this chapter, I argue for the use of case studies of peer institutions to understand the larger context, offering opportunities for IR professionals to attend to the interplay between technical, issues, and contextual intelligence. With the use of McGilchrist's (2009) metaphor of the divided brain, I explore how IR professionals will benefit from thinking about their work as using the two different hemispheres of the brain to develop the ability to focus both narrowly (left hemisphere) and broadly (right hemisphere) on particular issues of interest at their home institution.

NEW DIRECTIONS FOR INSTITUTIONAL RESEARCH, no. 174 © 2017 Wiley Periodicals, Inc.
Published online in Wiley Online Library (wileyonlinelibrary.com) • DOI: 10.1002/ir.20222

The Divided Brain

In his book, *The Master and His Emissary*, psychiatrist Iain McGilchrist (2009) cites society's misguided understanding of how the two hemispheres of the brain process information and stresses the need for a new interpretation. The enduring, though incorrect, narrative of what the hemispheres do states that language and reason occur primarily in the left hemisphere and creativity is confined to the right hemisphere. McGilchrist argues that we should move away from this false hypothesis and consider how the two hemispheres process information rather than what information they process: The types of attention the hemispheres engage in with a subject is more important than the subject. Most animals have a divided brain, in which the left hemisphere isolates pieces of information, while the right hemisphere addresses the context. A bird may activate its left hemisphere to locate seeds, while engaging its right hemisphere to maintain an awareness of potential predators, mates, or allies (McGilchrist, 2009). The two hemispheres cooperatively work together, using both the precise focus of the left and the broad contextual awareness of the right, for survival.

The left hemisphere processes information as pieces, and categorizes the information once it is stripped from its context. In this way, information processing is linear and sequential, where an individual breaks the whole into parts and then reconstructs the whole to explain what happened. Information processing of the left hemisphere is impersonal, but logical. The left hemisphere approach to data collection and analysis is reflective of the typical, mostly quantitative work of IR professionals. In survey data analysis, which may be considered as a left hemispheric approach, IR professionals take each data point for a singular response and create an aggregate to describe an average from the sample, thereby reconstructing the whole from the parts.

A left hemispheric approach to institutional research is a necessary approach to take. We need to have a process for understanding the complexities of an issue or problem. Technical and issues intelligence reside in the left hemisphere, demanding precise and targeted attention. Yet, taking the data out of their context to achieve precision in analysis is insufficient and problematic. "According to the left hemisphere, understanding is built up from the parts; one starts from one certainty, places another next to it, and advances as if building a wall, from the bottom up" (McGilchrist, 2009, p. 142). In a left hemispheric approach, IR professionals narrow their attention to isolated objects, a process that may be helpful in decision-making when looking for absolute or objective answers.

Qualitative research also has the tendency to be left hemisphere–centric at times. Most qualitative methodologies (e.g., narrative inquiry, ethnography, case study) employs a logical sequence to data collection and analysis. Conducting interviews or focus groups provide individual perspectives on a given issue, of which the researcher codes the data to identify larger thematic patterns. However, unlike quantitative research, qualitative re-search takes into the account the context of the issue or problem under study. In this way, qualitative research also engages the right hemisphere and seeks to achieve a balance between narrow and broad attention.

We need contextual understanding to engage in interpretation that is not explicit or literal (McGilchrist, 2009). The right hemisphere is less con-cerned about what the information is, and more immersed with how the information came to be. Instead of stripping the information away from its surroundings, the right hemisphere prefers wholeness of the informa-tion within its surroundings. Rather than focusing on a single object or as-pect, the right hemisphere attends to the object, its immediate background, and the global aspects of the setting concurrently. The right hemisphere ob-serves how pieces work together—or conflict with each other—concerning a single issue. McGilchrist speaks of how the right hemisphere plays a leading role in being present in the world. He states, "…the right hemi-sphere deals with the world before separation, division, analysis has trans-formed it into something else, before the left hemisphere has re-presented it" (McGilchrist, 2009, p. 179). Through the right hemisphere, we experi-ence the world in all its fluidity and interconnectedness; we are mindfully aware.

In day-to-day activities, the two hemispheres cooperate by actively in-hibiting the other's ability to engage in a task; in other words, they work together by working separately, as shown in the previous example of a bird looking for sustenance while maintaining an awareness of its surroundings. On an ontological level—how we view and make sense of our world—there is an imbalance in degree of cooperation. Ideally, the right hemisphere at-tempts to understand something beyond what is right in front of it, and the left hemisphere helps the right hemisphere achieve that end. To do so, the right hemisphere would first accept the information and send it to the left hemisphere for unpacking. The left hemisphere, in turn, would isolate the information for analysis and then return it back to the right hemisphere to make an integrated whole. Often, the right hemisphere sends the infor-mation to the left hemisphere for unpacking and there it stays. McGilchrist (2009) states, "Although the left hemisphere does not see and cannot under-stand what the right hemisphere understands, it is an expert at pretending it does, at finding quite plausible, but bogus, explanations for the evidence that does not fit its version of events" (p. 234).

We see this imbalance in institutional research at times, particularly when we analyze data out of their context to find a solution or direction for a decision. The tendency to use left hemispheric thinking is not wrong; it is the type of attention that offers a linear means of understanding data and a structure to explain the information. Right hemispheric attention, however, serves as the "mediator of experience" (McGilchrist, 2009, p. 227). After unpacking the information in the left hemisphere, the data must be returned to the right hemisphere to understand the information in its given context,

NEW DIRECTIONS FOR INSTITUTIONAL RESEARCH • DOI: 10.1002/ir

and is the primary argument for why contextual intelligence is critical for institutional research.

Cooperative Attention Framework

Practically speaking, how does an IR professional balance the interplay between contextual awareness, isolating important information, and grounding the information within its context for greater understanding? McGilchrist (2009) suggests thinking about the broad contextual awareness of the right hemisphere as living in the terrain, or the on-the-ground immediate experience of the lived world. When we inhabit the terrain, we stay present and alert to our surroundings. We engage in sense making to identify problems or opportunities (Weick, 1995) and continuously develop and grow our contextual intelligence. For IR professionals, inhabiting the terrain of the right hemisphere could mean noticing changes in common institutional inquiries (e.g., student enrollment, demographics, and faculty salaries) and sensing potential issues. Inhabiting the terrain provides institutional context.

In contrast, the precise narrow focus of the left hemisphere can be thought of as rising above the ground-level experience—a bird's eye view—existing in the territory. When we are in the territory, we separate ourselves from our immediate experience to observe what is happening to plan and strategize. As we move from the terrain to the territory, we engage our issues and technical intelligence because we begin to narrowly focus on an issue of interest for which we must collect information. For IR professionals, inhabiting the territory includes collecting qualitative data from focus groups, document analysis, and observations to understand an issue or problem. We can then use the data to plan or strategize a subsequent next step or decision needed to move forward. Finally, in a cooperative attention framework, the information gathered in the territory must be brought back to the terrain for contextual grounding. McGilchrist (2009) suggests thinking about the terrain of the right hemisphere and the territory of the left hemisphere as the x- and y-axes of a graph. In Figure 6.1, I have taken McGilchrist's concepts of the terrain and territory and applied it to Terenzini's (1993) technical, issues, and contextual intelligences; the line depicts the cooperative attention process of moving information from the terrain (gathering contextual information) to the territory (gathering issues and technical information) and then back to the terrain (for contextual grounding).

When Terenzini (1993) initially conceived of the idea that contextual intelligence was the most complex form of organizational intelligence an IR professional could develop, he viewed it from a cultural vantage point. Terenzini encouraged IR professionals to study the "organizational saga" (Clark, 1972), to learn about the institution's history, decision-making processes, and customs. Although briefly mentioning that knowledge of state, national, and international environments would be helpful in developing

Figure 6.1. Cooperative attention framework.

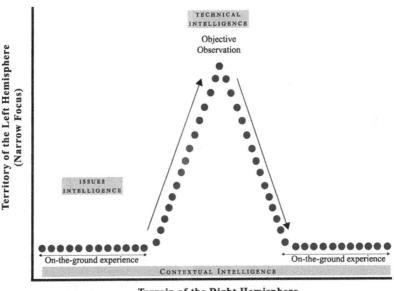

Terrain of the Right Hemisphere
(Broad Focus)

contextual intelligence, Terenzini focused more on peeling back the contextual layers within the institution where IR professionals work. From this perspective, the qualitative approach most applicable to identifying and understanding context is ethnography, a procedure of describing, analyzing, and interpreting a group's shared behaviors and beliefs (Creswell, 2012).

Thirty years later, Terenzini (2013) revisited his article and noted that his initial advice to learn the culture of the institution in order to develop contextual intelligence was naïve. Instead, he argued that developing contextual intelligence rests with maintaining an awareness of the national and international trends in higher education. For example, increased competition for external funding, one national trend, compels institutional leaders to think creatively, strategically, and intentionally about how new programs or initiatives could be attractive to potential individual, corporate, or foundation donors. Another trend is the increased competition for new students. IR professionals can play a leading role in calling attention to national trends concerning what institutional aspects are most marketable to prospective students and their families. Contextual understanding, therefore, becomes broader than what is happening at the home institution. Taking Terenzini's new knowledge in hand, IR professionals must explore the terrain of their own campus and the broader context of other campuses nationally or internationally with the right hemisphere, identify an issue of interest and gather data of the territory with the left hemisphere, and then ground the data in their context by returning the information back to the terrain of the right hemisphere. On an abstract level, the process mirrors the cooperative attention framework of information passing from the right hemisphere to the left hemisphere and back to the right hemisphere for an integrated approach to understanding a particular issue of interest. On a practical level, IR professionals can engage in such an activity with the use of qualitative case studies of peer institutions.

Using Case Studies of Peer Institutions in the Cooperative Attention Framework

Yin (2014) defines case study as an inquiry into a contemporary set of events that occurs in a real-world context and is bounded by time and place. The contemporary set of events may include a program or initiative that involves single individuals as well as a group of individuals (Merriam, 2009). Unlike other qualitative designs that are truly exploratory in nature (e.g., grounded theory, phenomenology, and narrative inquiry), case study is one qualitative method to choose when a researcher already has a solid understanding on a given issue and uses that understanding to identify patterns in institutional data that nationally normed surveys and other typical methods of gathering institutional data cannot provide.

Qualitative research questions ask how something (an event, a program, and a situation) came to be and why. Questions of "how" and "why" are grounded in right hemispheric thinking—they demand to know the context where the phenomenon exists or to understand the terrain using the right hemisphere. Once identified, IR professionals bound the case study by time and place, which helps to distinguish what data should be collected and examined and what data should be ignored. Bounding the case helps to isolate the data—using the left hemisphere to inhabit the territory—to make an abstract phenomenon concrete for examination. Data collection for case studies is similar to other qualitative designs discussed in Chapter 2 and analysis can employ deductive, inductive, or descriptive approaches. In writing a case-study report, or the findings, the data and analysis leave the territory and return to the terrain, or the right hemisphere, as contextualized data. I describe the process of moving from the terrain of the right hemisphere, to the territory of the left hemisphere, and back to the terrain of the right hemisphere to demonstrate the innate relationship case-study design has with the cooperative attention framework.

The description of the context is critical in the case-study report, yet there are varying characterizations of context. A common definition for context is the immediately relevant attributes of a phenomenon—the physical location, people involved, history, and cultural components (Lane, Brown, & Christopher, 2004; Miles & Huberman, 1994). McGilchrist (2009) understands context as the interrelations between subjects or phenomena. In writing the context or the terrain of a single case study, a researcher could describe the concrete environment where the case occurs, who is involved in the case, what actions those individuals took in relation to the case, and the interrelated meanings of those actions. The artifacts of the cultural context—language, ceremonies, technology, or certain curricular structures—are also information for the case (Lane et al., 2004). Context, defined as the physical, social, and behavioral environment where the phenomenon occurs, maps perfectly onto Terenzini's (1993) original conception of contextual intelligence. Yet, in revisiting his theory of contextual intelligence, Terenzini (2013) argues that the context stretches beyond the home institution, with the physical, social, and behavioral environment described from a national or international standpoint. According to Terenzini's revision, the terrain is vast. From this perspective, the use of case studies continues to be helpful in identifying and understanding the larger terrain. Case studies of peer institutions focused on a particular issue of interest can help an IR professional develop contextual awareness of the broader higher education landscape.

I pause here to clarify this peer institution approach. I do not mean for the IR professional to engage in a multi–case-study project, though that could certainly be an option if the IR office had the resources and time to engage in such a task. If so, Chapter 2 in this volume could certainly provide a technical overview of how to conduct such a study. Instead, I use the idea of case studies of peer institutions to determine how other universities and colleges are approaching the issue of interest, thereby creating an opportunity to gain greater contextual understanding beyond the home institution. Case studies, as they relate to developing contextual intelligence, are simply a strategy to gain knowledge of the larger higher education ecology. Many specialists in higher education, be it IR professionals, program developers, or administrators, instinctually engage in context-gathering activities. For example, administrators who are seeking external funding to develop a program on their campus will look at components of similar existing programs at other campuses, through talking with colleagues or researching online, to guide their own program development.

Identifying which peer institutions would offer the best case studies to provide contextual understanding requires purposeful sampling (Miles & Huberman, 1994). I suggest four possible approaches to take when selecting two to three case studies of peer institutions that would provide a broader context for the issue of interest. The first approach is to choose cases that reflect "maximum variation" within the larger context (Creswell, 2012; Miles & Huberman, 1994). For example, a research university, a liberal arts college, and a community college could provide a diverse range of contexts within which IR professionals could find common patterns. Jones and Braxton (2009) used a maximum variation sampling strategy to select eight states that earned the highest grades ($n = 4$) and lowest grades ($n = 4$) for "completion" on the Measuring Up 2006 National Report Card on Higher Education, and examined the activities each institution in those states engaged in to increase student persistence.

Conversely, a "homogeneous" sampling strategy would focus the broader context on a subset of peer institutions (Creswell, 2012; Miles & Huberman, 1994). If IR professionals' home institutions are liberal arts colleges, selecting peer institutions that are also liberal arts colleges would provide targeted contextual understanding. Location of institutions can also help determine a homogeneous sample. Lane et al. (2004) note that the unique characteristics of the geographical region affect the context of an institution. For example, urban and rural campuses create different institutional contexts, just as commuter and residential campuses differ.

Another approach would be to choose peer institutions as "critical" cases that could support broader generalization. Choosing critical cases is an effective approach if IR professionals are trying to learn about the types of contexts that would support the success of a particular initiative or program (Creswell, 2012; Miles & Huberman, 1994). Museus and Liverman (2010) used a critical case approach to identify three predominately White institutions that effectively and equitably retained and graduated underrepresented minority and White students in STEM. Museus and Liverman used IPEDS, the Education Trust's College Results Online (CRO) database, and the California Community Colleges Chancellor's Office Data Mart to select the peer institutions, based on their graduation- and retention-rate data.

The final approach is to select cases that would be "politically" important. Politically important cases attract desired attention (Miles & Huberman, 1994). In this scenario, IR professionals may want to choose peer institutions whose prospective faculty members or students overlap with their home institutions. Political sampling is useful if the issue of interest concerns admissions practices or other attributes that would make the home institution more marketable to prospective faculty members, students, and their families.

IR professionals can use case studies of peer institutions to develop contextual intelligence by engaging in the cooperative attention framework of right and left hemispheric thinking (McGilchrist, 2009). Recall from the previous discussion that the terrain of the right hemisphere is our on-the-ground experience of the lived world and an awareness to our surroundings. Like the example of the bird, working in the terrain creates an awareness of not only predators but also friends or allies. On the other hand, the territory of the left hemisphere observes the issue of interest; the territory allows for a narrow focus of the left hemisphere to collect information for analysis to plan for subsequent actions.

New-Faculty Orientation: Applying the Cooperative Attention Framework

When using a cooperative attention framework, IR professionals move from the right hemisphere where they engage in contextual grounding (terrain), to the left hemisphere (territory) to gather specific information, and return to the right hemisphere (terrain) to make sense of the data in their context. The application of the cooperative attention framework and use of case-study methodology to gain contextual understanding is a suitable approach to use for institution-wide initiatives like recruiting and retaining new faculty, as faculty retention and student retention are key institutional priorities.

Faculty play a critical role in student outcomes of persistence, retention, and completion (Hand, 2008). Research on early-career faculty retention and attitude toward the profession cite that new faculty find the tenure system problematic and unclear, perceive a lack of community with their peers, and feel a lack of integrated life between teaching and research, all of which lead to higher levels of dissatisfaction (Cullen & Harris, 2008). Targeted faculty retention efforts can begin in the first year with the development and implementation of a successful new-faculty orientation program. Yet, what comprises an effective orientation program that could address early-career faculty concerns around tenure, community, and teaching–research integration? The development of such a program is decisively context dependent.

IR professionals can be helpful to administrators tasked with faculty recruitment and retention by gathering both contextual intelligence at the home institution and from peer institutions, activating the terrain of the right hemisphere. At the home institution, engaging in sense making through identifying and understanding institutional culture is critical. This on-the-ground context may take the form of observing how the institution's mission, vision, and core values are spoken about by the current faculty. Moving into the territory of the left hemisphere and activating technical intelligence, IR professionals may also consider conducting focus groups with early-career faculty or administering surveys with open-ended questions at the home institution to gather data about early-career faculty members' experiences participating in new-faculty orientation, what parts of the program were helpful, and what information they wished was covered. The IR professional would then ground the data in the institutional context of the home campus, returning the information back to the terrain of the right hemisphere, which could potentially inform future modifications to new-faculty orientation at the home campus.

Gathering contextual intelligence by using case studies of peer institutions, however, provides a richer and broader understanding of new-faculty orientation. For example, how do administrators determine what constitutes a new-faculty orientation program? The formats of orientation programs can vary from a single day-long event to an intensive week-long program, to a single event held prior to the start of a semester with follow-up workshops held throughout the academic year (Schönwetter & Nazarko, 2008). Moreover, the topics covered in new-faculty orientation can range from role-specific areas like teaching, research, and service, to human-resource–focused topics, such as Title IX and sexual harassment policies. How do administrators determine which topics provide the best methods to socialize new faculty? Finally, the institutional unit that sponsors the event also provides context in terms of responsibility and ownership of supporting new faculty. Depending on the institution, the orientation sponsor may be the Office of Academic Affairs, Center for Teaching, Office of Research, Human Resources, or the individual deans of particular schools and colleges at larger institutions (Schönwetter & Nazarko, 2008). Thus, a case-study approach to understand the creation and implementation of a new-faculty orientation can offer greater insight into national efforts to support and retain new faculty.

To use a case-study approach to understanding peer institutions' new-faculty orientation programs, IR professionals may consider the four types of sampling frames previously articulated in this chapter. A "maximum variation" sample may include gathering contextual data about new-faculty orientation programs from a research-intensive university, a liberal arts college, and a comprehensive college to determine if there are any patterns to the topics covered, whereas a homogeneous sample of say, new-faculty orientation programs from HBCUs, might offer common programmatic themes that are not present from a wider, heterogeneous sample of institutions. If Centers for Teaching and Learning sponsor new-faculty orientation, identifying the Centers known for delivering quality education development programs, perhaps through the Professional and Organizational Development (POD) Network, could serve as "critical cases" to provide contextual understanding about best practices for orientation. Finally, identifying which institutions compete with the home institution in faculty recruitment could serve as a political sample, and an IR professional may gather contextual information on the types of programming supports these competitor institutions offer new faculty.

Once IR professionals identify the peer institutions that would provide additional contextual understanding, they can begin to gather information on each peer institution as an individual case study. At this point, IR professionals would switch to the territory of the left hemisphere, and use narrow focus and technical intelligence to gather information. Many institutions publish their new-faculty orientation programs on line, which is a convenient source of data about what topics the orientation program covered. Another source of information are the sponsors or facilitators of the orientation programs. A conversation with key informants at each institution about how they determined the orientation topics, why they felt those topics were important, or why they determined their format to new-faculty orientation (e.g., 1 day, week-long, and follow-up workshops) provides depth of understanding into program development that an online source could not offer. This contextual information of peer institutions returns to the terrain of the right hemisphere, where it is integrated with the context of the home institution (i.e., on-the-ground sense making of institutional culture and values).

NEW DIRECTIONS FOR INSTITUTIONAL RESEARCH • DOI: 10.1002/ir

Once IR professionals grasp a richer understanding of context, the terrain of the right hemisphere, as it relates to preparing and supporting new faculty, they can use this intelligence to inform data collection at the home institution and move into the territory of the left hemisphere, which again may include surveys with open-ended responses or focus groups with current faculty who are in their early years at the institution. The data collection, however, is deeply informed by the broader context of new-faculty orientation. For example, when discussing potential modifications to new-faculty orientation with current faulty who experience a previous iteration of the program at the home institution, IR professionals and administrators could propose alterations based on the information they gathered from peer institutions. From there, the IR professional would take the data from the territory of the left hemisphere and return it to the terrain of the right hemisphere to determine if the suggestions or potential modifications to the new-faculty orientation program make sense in the context of the home institution.

Note that the identification of peer institutions, collection of information with the use of a case-study approach, and grounding the peer institution data within the context of the home institution follows the process of the cooperative attention framework in Figure 6.1 of moving from the terrain, to the territory, and back to the terrain. In addition, using the integrated context of the home institution and peer institutions to inform data collection and the subsequent data analysis within the context of the home institution also follows the process of the cooperative attention framework in Figure 6.1.

Conclusion

Acknowledging the issue of interest and the context in which it appears is a core practice of qualitative research and an ongoing theme of this volume. In Chapter 2, a discussion about the use of thick, rich description not only provides a detailed account of the context but also elucidates on the nuances of the indirect interpretation qualitative researchers must make about the issue under study. Chapter 3 speaks to the validity of qualitative research, which must directly consider the context for the indirect interpretation to be credible. The strategies or approaches shared in a programmatic initiative will only be as effective as the context they are implemented in, as discussed in Chapter 4. A distinctive characteristic of the right hemisphere is the desire to identify specific examples within a given category, rather than the category alone (McGilchrist, 2009). Here, the right hemisphere is concerned with uniqueness and willingly seeks out contradictory evidence when analyzing information. The identification of difference within a given context, particularly the desire to highlight individual distinction, is an attribute of qualitative research and explored in Chapter 5 as it relates to institutionally minoritized student identities. Chapter 6 argues that administrators cannot understand the results of quantitative information without the contextual intelligence afforded by qualitative data, reflecting the right hemisphere's tendency to reach understanding of the whole before understanding the nature of the parts. In this chapter, the cooperative attention framework integrates the use of broad contextual understanding through the study of peer institutions with the narrow focus on data collection at the home institution order to understand particular issues of interest better. Qualitative data cannot be separated from their context and by taking context into account, IR professionals can make greater sense of the world they study.

References

Clark, B. R. (1972). The organizational saga in higher education. *Administrative Science Quarterly, 17*(2), 178–184.

Creswell, J. W. (2012). *Educational research: Planning, conducting, and evaluating quantitative and qualitative research* (4th ed.). New York, NY: Pearson.

Cullen, R., & Harris, M. (2008). Supporting new scholars: A learner-centered approach to new faculty orientation. *Florida Journal of Educational Administration & Policy, 2*(1), 17–28.

Hand, M. W. (2008). Formalized new-faculty orientation programs: Necessity or luxury? *Nurse Educator, 33*(2), 63–66.

Jones, W. A., & Braxton, J. M. (2009). Cataloging and comparing institutional efforts to increase student retention rates. *Journal of College Student Retention: Research, Theory & Practice, 11*(1), 123–139.

Lane, J. E., Brown, I. I., & Christopher, M. (2004). The importance of acknowledging context in institutional research. *New Directions for Institutional Research, 124*, 93–103. Retrieved from http://onlinelibrary.wiley.com/doi/10.1002/ir.134/full

McGilchrist, I. (2009). *The master and his emissary.* New Haven, CT: Yale University Press.

Merriam, S. B. (2009). *Qualitative research: A guide to design and implementation.* San Francisco, CA: Jossey-Bass.

Miles, M. B., & Huberman, A. B. (1994). *Qualitative data analysis* (2nd ed.). Thousand Oaks, CA: Sage.

Museus, S. D., & Liverman, D. (2010). High-performing institutions and their implications for studying underrepresented minority students in STEM. *New Directions for Institutional Research, 148*, 17–27.

Schönwetter, D., & Nazarko, O. (2008). Investing in our next generation: Overview of orientation and workshop programs for newly hired faculty in Canadian universities (Part 1). *The Journal of Faculty Development, 22*(3), 214–222.

Terenzini, P. T. (1993). On the nature of institutional research and the knowledge and skills it requires. *Research in Higher Education, 34*(1), 1–10.

Terenzini, P. T. (2013). "On the nature of institutional research" revisited: Plus ça change ...? *Research in Higher Education, 54*(2), 137–148.

Weick, K. E. (1995). *Sensemaking in organizations.* London, England: Sage.

Yin, R. K. (2014). *Case study research* (5th ed.). Los Angeles, CA: Sage.

BETHANY LISI is the director of Faculty Development Initiatives in the Institute for Teaching Excellence & Faculty Development at the University of Massachusetts Amherst and the former associate director of grants and lead collaborator in Hampshire College's Center for Teaching and Learning.

NEW DIRECTIONS FOR INSTITUTIONAL RESEARCH • DOI: 10.1002/ir

7

Framed by Terenzini's revision of his classic "On the nature of institutional research" article, this chapter offers concluding thoughts on the way in which technical/analytical, issues, and contextual types of awarenesses appeared across chapters in this volume. Moreover, it outlines how each chapter demonstrated how qualitative inquiry is integral, rather than additive, to the development of organizational intelligence.

Using Qualitative Inquiry to Promote Organizational Intelligence

Ezekiel Kimball, Karla I. Loya

Each of the chapters in this volume have commented on the many different ways in which qualitative inquiry can contribute to organizational intelligence. In so doing, they respond to the formulation of organizational intelligence Terenzini (1993) first offered in his classic article, "On the Nature of Institutional Research." Therein, Terenzini (1993) suggested that there were three "equally important and interdependent kinds of organizational intelligence" (p. 3): technical/analytical intelligence, issues intelligence, and contextual intelligence. Chapters in this volume address one of these types of intelligence specifically by exploring fundamental qualitative skills useful to institutional researchers.

However, even while framing the volume in this way, chapter authors produced chapters that respond not just to Terenzini's (1993) original formulation of organizational intelligence, but also to a reappraisal of the idea undertaken on the 20th anniversary of its first appearance. In this updated discussion of organizational intelligence, Terenzini (2013) reaffirmed the importance of developing discrete technical/analytic, issues, and contextual skills and awarenesses. However, the reframed conceptualization of organizational intelligence also emphasized the rapidly changing higher education world and clearly argued for a more expansive methodological toolkit to meet these demands. The chapters in this volume respond to this imperative because of qualitative inquiry's unique ability to adapt to new circumstances. In fact, our authors comment precisely on how qualitative approaches to institutional research work can provide just this sort of flexibility. Qualitative approaches are by definition emergent, interpretive,

NEW DIRECTIONS FOR INSTITUTIONAL RESEARCH, no. 174 © 2017 Wiley Periodicals, Inc.
Published online in Wiley Online Library (wileyonlinelibrary.com) • DOI: 10.1002/ir.20223

and naturalistic (Maxwell, 2012). As a result, they are uniquely well suited to respond to both the ambiguity and fluidity of contemporary higher education environments.

Emergence in Institutional Research

When qualitative researchers talk about the emergent nature of methods and analysis, they intend to convey that the precise mechanisms by which a study is conducted evolve in response to the researcher's developing understanding of phenomena being studied. In other words, since qualitative researchers seek a nuanced and contextualized view of complex phenomena, they also assume that their understanding of the project will develop over time. This framing is fundamentally consistent with Terenzini's (1993, 2013) discussion of technical/analytical intelligence. Terenzini (1993) called technical/analytical awareness "fundamental and foundational" (p. 4) to the competence of institutional researchers and suggested that it consisted largely of procedural proficiency. In his 2013 revision, he added a few more things to consider part of this type of awareness: the need to let a question's substance and importance guide the inquiry; the dangers of using any data set, technology, or tool just because it is there; and the need to find an alternative to increasingly low survey response rates. Qualitative approaches can help address these new demands for institutional researchers through an emergent design resulting in the construction of new data sets based on intentionally recruited participants.

The first two chapters in this volume illustrate how these goals can be achieved with the use of qualitative approaches to build technical/analytical awareness. First, George Mwangi and Bettencourt use a series of vignettes to highlight the complex design decisions that an institutional researcher must ponder as they seek to build organizational intelligence through qualitative methods. These considerations include choosing paradigms and methodologies, formulating questions, selecting tools for data collection and analysis, and addressing the issue of research quality. George Mwangi and Bettencourt respond to Terenzini's revised explanation of technical/analytical awareness by describing a qualitative decision-making process wherein the substance and importance of the question guide the process and the limitations of existing data sets are transcended through the pursuit of new data best suited to the question being addressed.

Rallis and Lawrence continue the conversation on technical/analytical intelligence in Chapter 2 by reminding the reader that good research is useful research. As such, they challenge traditional understandings of validity by arguing that integrity—which they broadly construe to include considerations of purpose, methodological rigor, and ethics—is a better criterion for evaluating research quality. In so doing, they call into question the long-running assumption that adherence to the procedural norms established by the quasi-canonical validity threat typology (Shadish, Cook, &

Campbell, 2002) will help produce meaningful research. Instead, they suggest that high-quality research can be produced only when a researcher thinks about both the norms established by their community of practice, which Rallis and Lawrence represent via the National Research Council's Scientific Principles for Education Research, and also how findings will be used. Notably, although they contextualize this argument primarily in qualitative work, they do not limit their claims regarding the centrality of integrity to qualitative work: instead, they suggest that research drawn from any methodological approach is ultimately evaluated based on its integrity. This argument is consistent with Terenzini's (2013) argument regarding the need for new methodological vistas and for research designs to be based on the underlying problem being studied.

Interpretation in Institutional Research

Qualitative researchers describe their work as interpretive in order to capture two fundamental truths: first, the goal of qualitative inquiry is learning; and second, in qualitative work, the researcher is always the instrument. As Terenzini (2013) sought to capture the evolving nature of issues awareness in the rapidly changing higher-education landscape, he framed the concept in interpretive terms. For example, Terenzini (2013) expressed concern about the capacity of institutions (and institutional researchers) to differentiate between good and bad ideas given the rapid proliferation of options in a technological age. As a result, he called upon institutional researchers to gain specialized expertise in a limited number of organizational areas (e.g., faculty work, enrollment management) and to use that expertise to "provide informed analysis and sound advice on alternative courses of action" (Terenzini, 2013, p. 147). Once again, qualitative research can help to meet this challenge as it has the unique potential to offer carefully considered information about both the status quo and potential paths forward.

In Chapter 3, Inkelas utilizes the results of a mixed-methods program assessment in order to demonstrate how qualitative methods provide key findings inaccessible via quantitative methods. She also shows that these findings produce actionable information about possible paths forward. In other words, Inkelas uses her discussion of both formative and summative assessment practices in order to show the limitations that could arise when using restricted methods to try to produce issues intelligence. Friedensen, McCrae, and Kimball pick up this same theme in Chapter 4. Their description of an unexpected finding related to the experiences of students with disabilities suggests that a single expected observation led them to view key elements of their broader study differently. Focusing on the interpretive dimensions of qualitative research, they argue that these findings would likely have been invisible in a standard quantitative design because of the innate tendency of measurement to restrict the researcher's point of view. The ability of qualitative research to pivot with the interpretation of researchers allows for issues intelligence to develop more organically, which is consistent with Terenzini's (2013) admonition to use the specialized expertise of institutional researchers to shape organizational learning.

Naturalism in Institutional Research

When qualitative researchers describe their work as naturalistic, they seek to explain that it is embedded in the context it seeks to describe. In much the same way, Terenzini (1993) intended contextual intelligence to capture the importance of environments. In his revision, however, Terenzini critiqued his original view of contextual intelligence "as still moderately accurate, but also as seriously parochial and naïve" (Terenzini, 2013, p. 144). In the revised version, Terenzini gives contextual intelligence a broader focus by including the broader landscape within which universities reside and threats to their operation such as eroding public confidence and declining appropriations. As a result, Terenzini (2013) summarizes this tier as including institutional, local, national, and even international awareness. He also suggests that contextual intelligence includes knowing how to navigate the political landscape for higher education and how to address demands for accountability. Although having this sort of holistic view is difficult in any research process, naturalism's underlying push toward understanding context means that qualitative research is well-suited to meet this challenge.

To that end, in Chapter 5, Williams and Stassen describe how a desire to understand context undergirded an institutional research office's decision to use both quantitative and qualitative tools in tandem. They note limitations of both approaches but establish the critical importance of qualitative methods in addressing questions of "How?" and "Why?" That is, in their case study, they suggest that qualitative data lend itself well to explanation. In so doing, Williams and Stassen establish the way in which multiple data points within a single institution might well be contextualized relative to one another with the use of qualitative methods. Lisi's Chapter 6 takes this contextualization a step further by building the case for the use of peer comparisons. Notably, Lisi provides both a compelling empirical demonstration of the utility of this work and also a description of the underlying psychological explanation for this type of work. In other words, she shows that contextualization is important for institutional research purposes and also that it stems from a fundamentally human impulse toward naturalistic inquiry.

The Case for Qualitative Inquiry

Throughout this volume, we have attempted to balance two separate-but-related narratives. The first narrative is a simple primer on qualitative inquiry in institutional research. Along with the talented authors who contributed to this volume, we hold that qualitative methods have great potential for institutional researchers. The chapters in this volume provide both concrete strategies for how to approach qualitative work in the context of institutional research and also compelling case studies for how others have done so. In this way, these chapters contribute to a small but meaningful literature base on qualitative methods in institutional research (e.g., Fetterman, 1991; Harper & Museus, 2007; Howard & Borland, 2001). This first narrative holds, as these other authors and editors have before us, that qualitative methods should be used more.

The second narrative is a bit subtler and ever so slightly subversive. We hold that not only should qualitative methods be used more often by institutional researchers but also that they *must* be used frequently in order to achieve organizational intelligence. To make this case, we summarize both Terenzini's three steps to organizational intelligence (technical/analytical, issues, and contextual) and the three main features of qualitative inquiry (emergence, interpretation, and naturalism).

As described above, qualitative inquiry is uniquely well suited to address the highly specific problems that arise in institutional research work. Terenzini (2013) noted in his redefinition of technical/analytic intelligence that new methods are required to meet these evolving needs. Qualitative research's emergent design means that its approach bends to the problem rather than forcing the problem to fit available data or methods. Rallis and Lawrence make a convincing case that we should be problem-focused in our evaluation of research quality, and George Mwangi and Bettencourt show the sort of rigorous, systematic decision-making supporting good qualitative work. Together, these chapters both argue that qualitative work can satisfy Terenzini's (2013) criteria for technical/analytic intelligence and also hint that some problems may require qualitative methods.

The idea that problems may require qualitative methods can also be seen clearly in the work of Inkelas as well as that of Friedensen, McCrae, and Kimball. They suggest that, as we seek to build toward Terenzini's (2013) issues intelligence, the need for nuanced information to support expert interpretation demands qualitative work in cases like those described in their chapters. Here, we go a step further: We suggest that qualitative research's fundamentally interpretive orientation to the world is well suited to meet the demands of a rapidly changing higher education environment. Although some problems may not require this degree of flexibility, it seems plausible to conclude that at some point, institutional researchers will be asked to make use of their expert knowledge to confront a problem for which ready quantitative data are unavailable or even impossible to obtain. In these situations, qualitative research represents the best (and perhaps only) path forward for the creation of organizational intelligence.

Finally, the naturalism of qualitative research is capable of capturing the loosely coupled nature of the nested systems that compromise contemporary higher education organizations. As Terenzini (2013) noted, the complexity of colleges and universities presents unique challenges in the development of contextual intelligence. Although sophisticated statistical techniques such as hierarchical linear modeling and econometric modeling do take into account multiple contextual influences, qualitative findings remain more approachable to the vast majority of potential users of institutional research findings. Institutional researchers seek to produce organizational intelligence in order to shape institutional action. As such, the ability of those who encounter institutional research findings to understand them matters a great deal. Here once again, qualitative work represents a meaningful way forward.

In making this argument, we do not wish to suggest that quantitative approaches to institutional research are unimportant. We wish only to make clear that qualitative approaches are as well, and not simply in an incidental, value-added way. Rather, our argument is that qualitative inquiry is central to the production of organizational intelligence. Viewed in this way, the limited treatment of qualitative inquiry in core texts used to orient new institutional researchers to the field (e.g., Howard, McLaughlin, & Knight, 2012; Knight, 2003) is particularly problematic as is the comparative scarcity of qualitative topics in core institutional research periodicals (such as Research in Higher Education, Professional Files, and Assessment Update). Our hope is that this volume is a first step in rectifying this inattention to the importance of qualitative methods.

References

Fetterman, D. M. (Ed.). (1991). Using qualitative methods in institutional research. *New Directions for Institutional Research, 72.*

Harper, S. R., & Museus, S. D. (Eds.). (2007). Using qualitative methods in institutional assessment. *New Directions for Institutional Research, 136.*

Howard, R. D., & Borland, K. W. (Eds.). (2001). Balancing qualitative and quantitative information for effective decision support. *New Directions for Institutional Research, 112.*

Howard, R. D., McLaughlin, G. W., & Knight, W. E. (Eds.). (2012). *The handbook of institutional research.* San Francisco, CA: Jossey-Bass.

Knight, W. E. (Ed.). (2003). *The primer for institutional research.* Tallahassee, FL: Association for Institutional Research.

Maxwell, J. A. (2012). *Qualitative research design: An interactive approach* (3rd ed.). Thousand Oakes, CA: Sage Publications.

Shadish, W. R., Cook, T. D., & Campbell, D. T. (2002). *Experimental and quasi-experimental designs for generalized causal inference* (2nd ed.). Belmont, CA: Wadsworth Publishing.

Terenzini, P. T. (1993). On the nature of institutional research and skills it requires. *Research in Higher Education, 34*(1), 1–10.

Terenzini, P. T. (2013). "On the nature of institutional research" revisited: Plus ça change …? *Research in Higher Education, 54*(2), 137–148.

EZEKIEL KIMBALL is an assistant professor of higher education at the University of Massachusetts Amherst.

KARLA I. LOYA is an assistant professor of educational leadership at the University of Hartford.

INDEX

NEW DIRECTIONS FOR INSTITUTIONAL RESEARCH

ORDER FORM SUBSCRIPTION AND SINGLE ISSUES

DISCOUNTED BACK ISSUES:

Use this form to receive 20% off all back issues of *New Directions for Institutional Research*.
All single issues priced at **$23.20** (normally $29.00)

TITLE	ISSUE NO.	ISBN

Call 1-800-835-6770 or see mailing instructions below. When calling, mention the promotional code JBNND to receive your discount. For a complete list of issues, please visit www.wiley.com/WileyCDA/WileyTitle/productCd-IR.html

SUBSCRIPTIONS: (1 YEAR, 4 ISSUES)

☐ New Order   ☐ Renewal

U.S.	☐ Individual: $89	☐ Institutional: $362
CANADA/MEXICO	☐ Individual: $89	☐ Institutional: $404
ALL OTHERS	☐ Individual: $113	☐ Institutional: $440

Call 1-800-835-6770 or see mailing and pricing instructions below.
Online subscriptions are available at www.onlinelibrary.wiley.com

ORDER TOTALS:

Issue / Subscription Amount: $ _____

Shipping Amount: $ _____
(for single issues only – subscription prices include shipping)

Total Amount: $ _____

SHIPPING CHARGES:

First Item $6.00
Each Add'l Item $2.00

(No sales tax for U.S. subscriptions. Canadian residents, add GST for subscription orders. Individual rate subscriptions must be paid by personal check or credit card. Individual rate subscriptions may not be resold as library copies.)

BILLING & SHIPPING INFORMATION:

☐ **PAYMENT ENCLOSED:** *(U.S. check or money order only. All payments must be in U.S. dollars.)*

☐ **CREDIT CARD:**   ☐ VISA   ☐ MC   ☐ AMEX

Card number _____Exp. Date _____

Card Holder Name_____Card Issue # _____

Signature _____Day Phone_____

☐ **BILL ME:** *(U.S. institutional orders only. Purchase order required.)*

Purchase order # _____
Federal Tax ID 13559302 • GST 89102-8052

Name_____

Address_____

Phone_____ E-mail_____

Copy or detach page and send to: **John Wiley & Sons, Inc. / Jossey Bass**
PO Box 55381
Boston, MA 02205-9850

PROMO JBNND